GLASS ENGRAVING

Barbara Norman

Foreword by David Peace

David & Charles
Newton Abbot   London
Charles E Tuttle Company : Publishers
Rutland, Vermont

British Library Cataloguing in Publication Data

Norman, Barbara
  Glass engraving.
  1. Glass engraving
  748.6   TT298

  ISBN 0–7153–8027–3

© Barbara Norman 1981

First published in Great Britain by David & Charles, 1981
Second impression, 1987

First published in the United States by Arco Publishing, Inc, 1981
This edition published by Charles E. Tuttle Co Inc, 1987

Photoset and printed in Great Britain
by Redwood Burn Limited, Trowbridge, Wiltshire
for David & Charles Publishers plc
Brunel House   Newton Abbot   Devon

ISBN 0–8048–7018–7 (United States)
Library of Congress
Catalog Card No. 87–50297 (United States)

Published by the Charles E. Tuttle Co Inc
of Rutland, Vermont & Tokyo, Japan
with editorial offices at
Suido 1-chome, 2-6, Bunkyo-ku, Tokyo, Japan

Contents

Foreword

I wonder which is the most important – judgement, experience or enthusiasm? Perhaps the last two together, one leading to the other. In this book, which has the very breath of enthusiasm, based on experience, Barbara Norman shows an underlying judgement which makes her advice appropriately level-headed. It is a very practical survey of a craft, remarkably comprehensive and is clearly addressed personally to the readers – you and me.

This is no lifeless lecture. Barbara Norman's eagerness is infectious. Indeed the craft of glass engraving seems to be spreading so rapidly in Britain and the USA that it is like good cheer spreading through a community; or more accurately, the craft is leading steadily to more people enjoying a cheerful, rewarding contentment in calmly achieving pleasing results – even works of art – at a time when part of the rest of the world seems to be going mad.

When the Guild of Glass Engravers was founded I was anxious that it should above all foster *creative design*, and that this should be based on a knowledge of the history of this centuries-old craft. So I am glad that this book stresses that glass engraving should not be treated just as a 'hobby' – with potentially shallow overtones for a leisure pursuit in which it is *excellence* that is pursued – and glad too that the history of glass is so clearly presented. If only history was always taught with such keenly personal interest.

Barbara Norman rightly emphasises the engraver's responsibility towards the glass itself. Engraving should never be a trivial activity: glass is a magical material and not one to be trifled with. Indeed I believe that one must approach each engraving task with such an attitude that leads to the result being regarded as worth treasuring by its eventual possessors for 1000 years. I am the happy possessor of a few

7

pieces of Roman glass, sixteen or eighteen centuries old, in which the perfection of shape is such that I share still the delight the makers felt at achieving that happy result. And with so permanent a material as glass, permanently marked by the engraver, there is no reason why today's standard of excellence should not be enjoyed for centuries. That should be our aim and our timescale.

Barbara Norman opens our eyes – 'Engraving leads you to think about the world around you in a different way and to see all kinds of objects literally in a new light.' And perhaps this is the book's most important message.

David Peace

Guild of Glass Engravers
London

Introduction

In writing this second book about engraving on glass, I have constantly had in mind those who would love to embark upon this absorbing craft but who live far from places where examples of engraving may be seen, and for whom this book may be the only help and guidance available. For them, I have tried to describe in some detail what work done by the different methods of engraving looks like and I hope these descriptions, combined with varied photographs, will be helpful. I have not used the word 'hobby'. Engraving is far more than that: it is a fine craft. I hope this book will be useful, too, to those already engraving and that it may, perhaps, provide some different ideas. Copper wheel engraving has not been included in the chapter on methods of work because my aim has been to deal only with types of engraving which, if necessary, can be done without a permanent workbench or special accommodation.

This time, as well as providing information about engraving itself, there are chapters with suggestions for photographing engraved glass, exhibiting it and packing it.

Chapter 6 is about people: engravers themselves. I hope it conveys even a fraction of the enthusiasm for the craft and the enjoyment experienced by engravers which are everywhere so evident. Above all I hope it will encourage those starting this craft to know how other people have progressed.

Barbara Norman

1
The Development of Engraving

For many centuries after its discovery, glass was regarded as a luxury and it was a natural development of this idea that glass should either be used as a means of decoration or should itself be decorated. Indeed, the oldest surviving pieces of glass, found in Egypt, are decorative objects: beads and small amulets. Glass was incorporated into lavish gold jewellery by the Egyptians and pieces of coloured glass were used to make mosaic bowls. Mosaics on floors and walls, too, were sometimes made with glass.

The simplest way of decorating glass was to colour it. Another way was to engrave it and at first this was done by lapidary workers who were able to adapt their methods of cutting and polishing stones to engraving and polishing glass. The Romans used this method of engraving, notably on the Portland Vase. They also used sharp tools for incising engravings.

So if you wish to start engraving today you will be carrying on an ancient craft, not starting off on some new idea which may or may not last. The craft of engraving has endured for many centuries but it has developed as well. The composition of glass itself has changed and the types of tools available nowadays are immensely more varied than those in use in ancient times.

Throughout its long history there have been periods when engraving was a popular means of decoration and then times when the demand for it declined in favour of other methods of decoration. But whatever the demand, it has often played a small but interesting part in recording historical events or reflecting contemporary tastes. Subjects for engravings have included commemorative works of many kinds: military events, anniversaries, royal emblems – including illegal Jacobite subjects – new bridges, buildings, ships.

This book has been written to enable people to engrave by methods which need the least equipment and are thus best suited to an ordinary home environment. But it would be a narrow approach when outlining the long history of engraving not to include some mention and description of other techniques as well. For this reason, reference is made to a very important branch of engraving – that done by the copper wheel method. It is always interesting, and often useful, for an engraver to be able to recognise the method which has been used to produce a particular piece of work. The effects obtained by one method cannot be exactly reproduced by another and you should never seek to copy anyone else's work, but nevertheless you may find your ideas developing by studying other methods of work.

In such work as the Portland Vase (described in Chapter 7) the Romans brought the craft of wheel engraving to a very high level. The principal characteristic of this method of work is that it creates a sculptured effect by grinding quite deeply into the glass. In the early stages of the work the whole surface of the engraving is matt, with little indication of light and shade. Shadow is then introduced by means of polishing. This eliminates, where desired, the whiteness of the original engraving. Another particularly Roman method of engraving was that used to produce the famous cage-cups, where the engraving is burrowed out so deeply that the intricate designs stand away from the cup, forming outer cage of glass.

After such a distinguished early history, engraving, like so much else, went into decline for several centuries during the Dark Ages. Eventually it emerged once more at the time when Venice reached its peak as a centre of glassmaking.

In their search for a clear glass which would resemble rock crystal the Venetians succeeded in producing cristallo, which is described more fully on page 162. This thin, brittle glass was unsuited to the copper wheel method of engraving which can cut quite deeply into glass. However, it was well suited to engraving done with fine diamond tools, and as Venetian glassmaking methods spread through Europe, people began to engrave this glass with diamonds. A variety of glass shapes were engraved: goblets, shallow dishes, bowls. The method involved working with lines and using cross-hatching in many attractive ways. The fine lines of the engraved decoration give a delicate appearance to the glass. By the mid-sixteenth century there were important centres of diamond point engraving in the Netherlands and in Germany and Austria. Choice of subject was varied and ambitious. There were floral designs, animals, coats of arms, ornate calligraphic designs. One famous goblet engraved in the first part of the seventeenth century shows a great panoramic view of the city of Mainz, as well as many ecclesiastical coats of arms and a long inscription – all on one goblet! The linear work used in this intricate design produces a fine, lacy appearance, in spite of the solidity of the subject-matter.

Diamond point engraving was introduced into England by Verzelini in the latter part of the sixteenth century and the engraving done on the few Verzelini goblets which survive is thought to have been done by Anthony de Lisle. De Lisle was a Frenchman who settled in England and eventually became naturalised. It is known that he was an engraver on pewter, and two of the surviving Verzelini goblets bear the engraved motto of the Pewterer's Company of London: 'In God Is All Mi Trust'. This is generally thought to provide a sufficient link with de Lisle for the engravings to be his.

During the sixteenth and seventeenth centuries diamond engraving in Holland won considerable fame, and the Dutch became known as great decorators of glass. First, during the seventeenth century there were the line engravings. Engravers were often amateurs and sometimes worked in groups. This must have been a delightful way of spending some leisure hours. It is interesting to note that there were three women among well-known engravers of the time. These were Anna Roemers Visscher, her sister, Maria Tesselschade Roemers Visscher, and Anna Maria van Schurman. Anna Roemers Visscher is best known for her wonderful calligraphic work. The calligraphy, although beautiful in itself, is primarily used to form a decorative pattern which completely encircles a goblet. She did not confine her work to this style, though, but also used fruit and flowers as subjects. Her sister, Maria Tesselschade Roemers Visscher, and Anna Maria van Schurman did similar work. They may have found engraving a more convenient form of art to practise in conjunction with busy domestic lives than, say, painting. They needed little equipment, no studio, and the small scale of the work was akin to other feminine craftwork such as embroidery or lacemaking.

Another well-known engraver of the period was Willem Jacobsz van Heemskerk who specialised in calligraphic designs. He was an interesting man, combining his great technical skill and artistic ability with many other activities. He was a cloth merchant of Leyden and also a poet and dramatist.

Eventually the use of diamond tools to produce linear engravings changed in favour of a different style of work: that of stipple engraving. It is thought that probably the first to use this method of work was Anna Roemers Visscher who stippled a cherry as part of a design. The use of tiny dots instead of lines was a change which led to the golden age of Dutch engraving in the eighteenth century.

During the latter part of the seventeenth century the early difficulties experienced in making the newly-discovered lead crystal had been overcome so that at the same moment as the new method of engraving was gaining in popularity the most suitable kind of glass was being made. Stipple engraving is at its best when done on good lead crystal – there is less likelihood that the glass itself will splinter, there is greater scope for fine gradations in light and shade, and the finished work has a faint luminosity which is unobtainable on soda glass.

There were many stipple engravers working in Holland in the eighteenth century and they frequently worked on lead crystal imported from England – much of it from Newcastle. Their work shows the art of stipple engraving at its peak. It is so fine that it looks almost like a fine film of steam on the glass. In some cases it is so fugitive that it seems as if the glass has no engraving on it at all. Then, by holding it to light at the right angle, you suddenly see this exquisite work. No lines have been drawn; everything is indicated by fine, tiny dots. Curves are accurate, lines – although stippled – are perfectly straight. Everything is precise and very delicate. Subjects vary widely and nothing seems to have been too intricate. Designs were often based on contemporary prints and this involved engraving human figures either in complicated settings or in clothes such as uniforms or flowing robes which must have presented technical problems. Even the reduction in size from the original to fit the infinitely smaller glass has been expertly done, since many of these engravings are on wineglasses rather than large goblets. Some engravers excelled in portraits; some produced heraldic designs.

Among the many gifted engravers of the period some stand out above their contemporaries. Frans Greenwood, who was Dutch in spite of his English name, lived from 1680–1761. He was born in

Rotterdam but worked in Dordrecht from 1726. Greenwood was the first engraver to work wholly by the stipple method, and the earliest recorded example of his work, a wineglass, dates from 1722.

The name of David Wolff (1732–1798) is another on the list of great Dutch engravers. He, too, worked by the stipple method and his fame was such that more work has been ascribed to him than he could have produced. Not much is known of him as a person. He is thought to have been born in 'sHertogenbosch and his father was probably Swiss. The subjects he chose were often complicated and he used stipple ingeniously. For instance, the branches and leaves of a tree were left blank and unengraved while the background was closely stippled, thus providing a white background. As the twigs and leaves were necessarily very tiny this called for great skill.

Aert Schouman (1710–1792) was probably one of Greenwood's pupils. Schouman was already an artist, being a water-colourist and a well-known decorator and copyist. He studied with the painter Adriann van der Burgh and when van der Burgh died in 1733, Schouman himself set up as a teacher and artist. His work was popular enough for it to be reproduced by contemporary engravers. His decorative work included such things as murals, fans and clock dials, so it was only a short step to decorating yet another medium – glass.

Other names to single out among the Dutch stipple engravers are G. H. Hoolart, who was a nephew of Frans Greenwood, and J. van den Blijk. Andries Melort carried this style of work well on into the nineteenth century.

A list of museums where engraved glass may be seen is included in the Appendix. An especially splendid collection of Dutch work may be seen in the Rijksmuseum in Amsterdam.

Holland usually comes to mind first as the home of diamond point engraving, but the craft also flourished in certain parts of Germany and Austria. Some of the earliest diamond engraved glasses were produced at Hall in Tirol, in about 1550, and the great wheel engraver, Georg Schwanhardt of Nuremberg, used a diamond point to emphasise certain parts of his wheel engravings. He also practised diamond point engraving by itself and his skill was such that he was summoned to Regensburg by the Emperor Ferdinand III in order to teach him to engrave.

On the whole, other methods of glass decoration, such as painting or wheel engraving were more popular in Germany, but diamond point engraving was practised in three places: Nuremberg, Saxony and Silesia. The work is mostly anonymous and much of it is in the form of armorial bearings. However, in the seventeenth century three names stand out: Peter Wolff of Cologne, August Otto Ernst von dem Busch who was a canon of Hildesheim, and C. A. F. Werther also from Cologne. Canon von dem Busch has been described as 'an impassioned amateur' and he apparently blackened his engravings with soot in order to make them more visible!

During the seventeenth century many English political events were commemorated by diamond point engravings. The most sought after are those known as Jacobite and Williamite glasses. The Jacobite glasses were engraved in support of the Stuart cause and were made within the comparatively short period of about 1745–1765. To be a Jacobite and to support the claims of the Stuarts to the throne was treasonable so even the existence of such glasses added a certain excitement to the times. Many of them were engraved with special emblems for some of the many secret clubs and societies which supported the Stuarts. Sometimes the treasonable nature of the designs was hidden behind the otherwise harmless designs. Well-known Jacobite emblems included the rose, a thistle, an oak leaf, a star, a blackbird, a bee and a cobweb – all having their particular complicated significance while at the same time being acceptable designs for engraving. Sometimes, however, the message was unmistakable when it took the form of actual words. In this group are glasses engraved with *Fiat* (May it happen), *Redeat* (May he return), and various other inscriptions. In a class by themselves are the famous 'Amen' glasses. These were obviously treasonable as they are engraved with all or part of the Jacobite anthem and include the word 'Amen'. They are now very rare and are much sought after. Because of their scarcity and interest they also attract forgers.

As a kind of counterstroke to glasses supporting the Stuarts there were also those engraved in support of William III, known now as Williamite glasses. These were all done by the copper wheel method and the subject-matter is rather more pedestrian than that of the more daring Jacobite glasses. Whereas the Jacobite engravings were interestingly secretive and rather tortuous in their interpretation, the Williamite ones are mostly portaits of William or long toasts, all written out fully.

While diamond point stipple engraving was flourishing so splendidly, the much bolder method of engraving with copper wheels was once more being revived, and this time primarily in Germany, Austria and Bohemia. As with diamond point engraving, the spread of the manufacture of the new lead crystal led to the revival of copper wheel engraving. As already mentioned, this method of work needed glass that was thicker and less brittle than Venetian cristallo. It is best done on soft, clear glass such as lead crystal as this responds so well to the essential polishing on parts of the engraving.

Copper wheel engraving developed from the craft of the lapidary, which in turn had been used on rock crystal in the absence of suitable clear glass. So in the seventeenth century everything came together: the ancient skills were already in existence and added to them was the right medium for the work – lead crystal.

Copper wheel engraving seems to have suited the German and Bohemian tastes more than diamond point. It is bolder in effect and can be splendidly ornate.

The first of the great engravers who worked at this period was Caspar Lehmann (1570–1622). He learnt glass engraving in Munich and worked there for two years at the court of Duke Wilhelm V. One of his contemporaries, Joachin von Sanrart, described him as the inventor of copper wheel engraving. Another of the great German engravers was George Schwanhardt of Nuremberg. In 1618, at the age of seventeen, he went to Prague to join the workshop of Lehmann as an apprentice, and when Lehmann died only four years later Schwanhardt inherited Lehmann's imperial privileges. He then returned to Nuremberg to work, and that city became a centre for wheel engraving.

Lehmann and Schwanhardt can be numbered in a long list of great wheel engravers. To name only a few others, there were Johann Wolfgang Schmidt, Hermann Schwinger, Hans Stefan Schmidt. But of the beautiful work of that period far more is unsigned than is signed, which simply shows how great was the revival of the craft.

Wheel engraving continued to grow during the nineteenth century and today there are very fine Czech, German, British and American craftsmen. At the time of writing there has been both a great development and a great revival of engraved glass, each taking place on different sides of the Atlantic.

First, the development, which concerns the art (or craft) of copper wheel engraving: this is taking place in the USA at Steuben Glass and is described on page 170.

The revival which is so excitingly taking place today concerns engraving in Britain. There is an ever-growing interest in engraved glass of all kinds. It is frequently written about in magazines and newspapers; it is the subject of television programmes; galleries are interested in showing it; and, above all, the general public is increasingly realising its value. The ever-rising price of silver has certainly resulted in more and more people choosing a piece of engraved glass as a commemorative present and in firms and institutions commissioning engraved glass for presentations. When I wrote my previous book in 1972 the craft was not practised widely. There was not much information available for those wanting to find out more about it and there was nothing which gave basic facts on how to start engraving. It was not easy to see hand-engraved glass other than in museums and there were few classes where the craft was taught. However, there was already a lot of interest in the subject.

One of the things which really turned the scales and speeded up this great revival was the founding of the Guild of Glass Engravers. As described on page 122 the Guild was the outcome of a hope by two friends, Elaine Freed and Elly Eliades, to try to persuade engravers to join together in some kind of society which would encourage an exchange of ideas and information. The craft was totally without a central point of reference, the interests of engravers were unrepresented, and although public interest in engraved glass was growing there was general unawareness of the craft.

Thanks to the great efforts and hard work of a small, dedicated group of people, both practising engravers and those simply interested in the craft, the Guild of Glass Engravers, formed in 1975, has gone from strength to strength. It has organised magnificent exhibitions of members' work; its annual meetings are thronged with members from every part of Britain; a fine quarterly journal is sent to members which not only gives much interesting and useful information about engraving and engravers in general, but also gives constant news about developments in tools and equipment. So keen were members to feel part of a body devoted to their own craft that three regional branches of the Guild have sprung up – in Sussex, East Anglia and the Chilterns. The Guild as a whole has members in the USA, Canada, Australia and the Continent of Europe. It recognises the value of engraving to people who are disabled and is pre-pared to support Guild members in instruction projects for the handicapped.

When the British revival of hand engraving is looked back on in time to come, the part played by the Guild of Glass Engravers will be seen to have been of the utmost importance.

2
Engraving:
Some Methods of Working

Hand engraving on glass proves to be, for almost everyone who embarks upon it, a most satisfying and absorbing craft. Indeed, there appear to be very few who discover they have no aptitude for it or who do not derive great pleasure from the work. It is creative and it is an ideal combination of art and craft.

To some people engraving sounds like a new and unusual craft. It may perhaps still be thought a little unusual but it is certainly not new, as was shown in the preceding chapter. Anyone who practises it now is continuing a craft which is many thousands of years old, and the idea of continuity and a link with craftsmen through the centuries surely gives an added interest. The work of those craftsmen of past centuries is a continual inspiration to modern engravers.

I find that people are always curious to know why an engraver ever gets started on this work, and there must surely be many answers to this question. Sometimes it is because someone has seen a piece of hand-engraved glass and has been instantly captivated by its beauty. This is what happened to me, and so unexpectedly too. I found myself thinking about commissioning some engraved glasses as a present. This was itself an unlikely situation as I had never before considered commissioning anything at all. However, the idea eventually led to my seeing some diamond point stipple engraving for the first time, done by Claire Rome, and I knew at once that I wanted to try to do this myself. It was just a sudden conviction and I have never ceased to be totally enthralled by the work. I always think how fortunate I was to have seen this beautiful engraving and so to have been able to start, myself, upon what have been years of immensely enjoyable work. Many people have been inspired in the same way because, now, there are so many more opportunities to see engraved glass in exhibitions. However, not everyone can manage to see any work and many just bravely start off on their own, aided only by photographs and descriptions.

Engravers are drawn from a wide variety of people, as is at once clear in any gathering of members of the Guild of Glass Engravers. They may be professional artists or craftsmen in other fields – painters, calligraphers, graphic designers – or their daily work may have no connexion at all with anything artistic or creative. Some discover the pleasures of engraving in retirement. Their common link is that they all greatly enjoy engraving.

Some of the foregoing may have given the impression that hand engraving on glass is too huge and ambitious a thing upon which to embark, is too expensive, or demands a great deal of space and costly equipment. Happily this is not so. Like any craft, or indeed almost any activity of any kind, you can go on spending money on it almost limitlessly. But the important thing about engraving on glass is that you *need not* spend too much on it. You can make just as much or as little of engraving as you wish or can afford. You can limit yourself to the simplest and cheapest hand tool and to reasonably priced, ordinary domestic glassware, and be content to do very simple, basic designs. They need be none the less pleasing or successful because they are simple. Or you can begin to build up a small range of better tools, get some lead crystal and embark upon more ambitious subjects. Whatever engraving you do will be unique – a one-off – and it will be something only you could create.

If you are very lucky you might be able to have a workroom or studio where you can spread all your reference books and equipment round you and not continually have to clear them away. But if this is not possible do not worry: it is a luxury and is not *essential*. A very wide range of work can be done in the ordinary conditions present in any home. You just need some suitable surface upon which to work and this need not necessarily be a table if you are doing diamond point work. Indeed, some people actually prefer to work on a cushion resting upon their knees. Of course, you need to be able to see your work clearly in whatever lighting conditions suit you personally. These are the simplest, basic requirements. If you are able to provide yourself with different, and better, conditions that is obvi-

21

ously an advantage. However, you need not feel hesitant about embarking upon engraving because some kind of special work-space seems too difficult to achieve.

The fact that no special workshop is an absolute necessity does, of course, prove a great advantage for those who are engraving in what may be very limited free time because, with almost nothing to set up beforehand, you can begin work at once and use every moment you have for actually doing the work. It may be only half an hour, but it is amazing how much can be done in a short time if that is all you can spare. In the end, all those precious moments snatched from your everyday tasks do mount up and suddenly you find you have finished work in your hand.

Some people are unsure about starting to engrave because they feel they cannot draw. Of course, it would be misleading to deny that an ability to draw, however modest it may be, is a great help. But the important thing to realise is that it is not *essential*. It simply depends upon what kind of work you want to do. There is a very wide range of work that can be done without the slightest need to draw creatively. For example, any kind of non-representational subject. This can be something geometrical. Or you may have seen some printed pattern or motif in a book or magazine. This can be traced on to the glass. Or you may want to concentrate on lettering, which can also be traced if necessary. Some very successful contemporary engravers have no hesitation in saying they are quite unable to draw or to do their own lettering – so take courage from this!

Another attraction of engraving is that it is companionable work, as was mentioned earlier in connexion with engravers in Holland in the seventeenth century. After writing my previous book, I had many letters from people who were caring for disabled or sick members of their families with whom they wished to spend their leisure hours instead of retreating to a separate workroom. For them, engraving was often a real blessing. It provided something entirely new, something immensely creative and something which could be done in their everyday surroundings – a little at a time if necessary. In some instances family interest in the work led to a pooling of ideas for designs, thus fully involving a disabled person in creative work.

Engraving leads you to think about the world around you in a different way and to see all kinds of objects literally in a new light. This is what engraving is all about: the portrayal of light. (The dark parts are left unengraved.) Therefore, once you start to think of things from the point of view of engraving you see the light on them or in them. You think in terms of illumination and of contrasts between light and dark areas. Objects form patterns of which you were previously unaware. When you have finished engraving a goblet you have, as it were, illuminated it.

Engravers are fortunate because they work on interesting and, usually, beautiful material: glass. So choosing and handling the base for your work, even before you take the first step towards the actual engraving, can in itself be a great satisfaction and pleasure. Working on glass, however, does carry a certain responsibility towards the glass itself. You have before you a vessel which has been designed and made to be a satisfying object in its own right; much thought has been given to its shape and proportions; much care has been taken in making it. An engraver should endeavour to ensure that the glass upon which he engraves is enhanced and not defaced by his work. When you first start to engrave, you will inevitably think almost wholly of how you can portray your chosen subject in terms of engraving. But later on, when you are more sure of technique and have a better idea of the results you want to achieve, you will start to think of matching a particular design to an appropriate shape of glass and that is when you can aim to end up with a good engraving which has actually complemented the piece of glass upon which you have worked.

Engravers, like many other craftsmen, have the choice of either doing work which is solely for visual pleasure and not for use, or decorating something made for use. The former may test the delicacy of your engraving; the latter may lead you to think of a stronger style of work with more visual impact. You may find you prefer working always in one way and not another. Many engravers settle for one style of work and this can have the advantage of enabling you to streamline the number and type of tools you need. But the opportunity for a great variety of work is always there.

Subjects for Engraving

I think one important contributing factor to the interest an engraver derives from the work is that the choice of subject-matter often involves much questioning and research. Suppose you have decided upon a design of some plant or flower. If you are lucky – and if it is the right time of year too – you may have an example in your garden. But if not (and this probably applies to most people) books on gardening or botany will have to be consulted. Having found enough detail about your chosen plant, can you adapt its shape satisfactorily to the glass upon which you want to engrave it? For example, you cannot engrave a tall, straight-stemmed flower with long, straight leaves, such as an iris, on a short, round glass. It will look right on a tall, slender glass. But if the flower itself is what interests you then that alone might look well on a smaller shape.

The same problems apply to almost anything else you can think of. Animals for example: how do they walk, sit, stand? Where is the centre of balance? What is the size of the head in proportion to the body? Another important point is what is their natural habitat? Is it possible to show them amidst the correct plants, grasses or trees? Animals are always interesting because, unlike many plants, their shape cannot be so well adapted to suit the shape of the glass. You have to try to find a realistic position for the animal which is in harmony with the lines of the glass – for example, tall animals on tall decanters; short, wide animals on short, broad glasses. Birds are interesting too. How do their various feathers differ in texture and in what surroundings do you find them? You may be asked to work out a design which commemorates someone's interest in sailing, for example, or fishing, and you may know nothing about either. More research! You may want to engrave some historical scene: how did people dress at the time? Off you go to the library to consult books of costume. Someone's pet dog is to be engraved on a goblet. You hardly knew the breed existed and all you have been supplied with is a small, murky photograph which gives no hint of light and shade, shows no bone structure and is quite useless. Again, your local library probably comes to the rescue and with a little effort you can build up a satisfactory picture of the animal.

Many engravers have to build up designs from reference books. Good, clear photographs give the best information. But right from the start you should try to avoid actually copying anything. For example, use a reference book about flowers as a source of information on their general shape, number of petals and so on, but after that, work out your own design. One important point is, I think, that you should never work from a drawing done by someone else.

24

That is totally uncreative and unsatisfying. The only exception might be if you were engraving something like an historic portrait. After all, you couldn't get a photograph of Shakespeare!

So once you start engraving you are learning all the time. All this searching round for information constantly opens up new paths of interest. Almost unconsciously, you find you are adding to your knowledge of things past and present to an extent which you would probably not otherwise be doing. Also, you build up a fund of knowledge on where to obtain information. It is quite a bonus in everyday life to know at once what are the sources of information on a great many things.

Once you become involved with engraving, you will find yourself always on the look-out for new ideas. You become more observant and inventive, and much more aware of good and bad design in general. It is impossible to say which way round things happen first: the discovery of a piece of glass which you find particularly pleasing and which you realise you very much want to engrave, or an idea for the subject of an engraving without knowing exactly upon what kind of glass you will actually do the work. Either way round, the search is enjoyable. Sometimes a piece of glass immediately conjures up in your mind a picture of what would be a splendidly appropriate engraving and you can hardly wait to start work on it.

At the designing stage there is always something to think about. It may be trying to think of a new subject: wondering where to get essential information about it. Or it may be the sudden solution to a technical problem. It is amazing how bright ideas for solving problems occur like bolts from the blue – usually when you are far away from engraving. It is often helpful to make a note of them at the time, though – ideas can vanish as quickly as they appear!

Methods of Engraving

Three methods of engraving glass by hand are described in this book: with a hand-held diamond or tungsten carbide tool (referred to here as diamond point engraving); with a flexible drive drill or dental drill, and dental burrs (referred to here as drill engraving); and with a Burgess Engraver. Each method may be used on its own, or it may be combined with either or both of the other methods in any way you wish. However, because of its use by many manufacturers of glass, the most easily recognised method of engraving is that done by copper wheels. Because so much of this is done commercially, this is probably the only kind of engraved glass most people have seen. For the reasons explained previously, this book does not deal with copper wheel engraving.

However, although no one would surely wish to imitate so great a craft by using other tools to try to produce similar work, there are certain effects obtained by copper wheels which can be adapted for use with different tools. This applies particularly to polishing parts of an engraving and will be dealt with later.

Although each of the three methods of hand engraving will be explained in detail, it might be useful to say here that, in general, diamond point engraving is delicate in appearance; drill engraving is, on the whole, more emphatic; and work done with a Burgess Engraver can either be very similar to diamond point or have as much strength as that done with a drill.

Types of Glass

The reasons for choosing a particular piece of glass upon which to work may be many. But first of all it helps to know exactly what is meant by the different descriptions of glass because you cannot always rely upon sales staff really knowing this.

Glass either contains lead or it does not. If it does not (ie if it contains soda lime instead) it is known as 'soda glass', and it is cheaper than glass containing lead. Most ordinary domestic glassware is made of soda glass. It tends to be fairly hard, but the degree of hardness does vary as between different manufacturers. Some soda glass can also be a little brittle. However, if it is all you can afford or all that is available to you, it is possible to do work that is not too complicated or ambitious by using a simple hand tool, a drill or a Burgess Engraver. Worked on in the right way, soda glass responds well.

When glass contains lead it is much softer – the more lead the softer the glass – and the addition of lead puts it into the category of crystal. It is the word 'crystal' which needs some explanation. According to the British Standard, that with the lowest lead content is described as Crystal Glass and must contain at least 10 per cent lead oxide or similar material. For glass to be described as Lead Crystal the raw materials from which it is made must contain at least 24 per cent lead oxide. At the top of the scale is Full Lead Crystal which must contain at least 30 per cent lead oxide. So do not be misled by someone talking encouragingly of 'crystal': the word can mean several things! As well as being the softest of the three grades of crystal, full lead crystal is also the most expensive.

So, to sum up the uses of the various kinds of glass: most soda glass is suitable for linear work with a diamond or tungsten carbide tool. Some of it can also take stippling if this is not too delicate. (If you have to bang at this, abandon stippling on that piece of glass; it will ruin your tools.) Soda glass is suitable for drill engraving and also for a Burgess Engraver. Proceed with care until you discover the texture of the glass. All categories of crystal are suitable for all types of work, although very fine stippling requires full lead crystal. Engraving done on coloured glass always shows up as pearly grey, no matter what the colour of the glass. As a bold effect is needed in order to get enough contrast between the pearly engraving and the colour of the glass, the work usually has to be done with a drill. That being so, it is not necessary to question the lead content of the glass.

Finally, some mention should be made of optical glass. This is hard and is more suited to electrical methods of work than to hand tools. It can be obtained from optical works in a variety of interesting shapes, usually unpolished – however, many optical works are willing to polish it as required.

Choosing Glass

When buying glass you may have difficulty in getting the correct information about its lead content, if any. However, you can go a long way yourself towards discovering this. You can quickly learn to tell the difference between soda glass and any kind of crystal mainly by its appearance. When placed beside lead crystal, soda glass has less clarity and brilliance and sometimes has a faint greenish tinge. However, a sure test is gently to 'ring' the glass with your fingernail. Soda glass makes a dull sound; crystal gives a distinctive ringing sound which increases with the amount of lead it contains. Full lead crystal can ring for several seconds. (Doing this for yourself in a shop is not always popular!)

The next question is where to find the glass you need. Soda glass should be no problem as there is more of it than anything else, and much of it is of pleasing design. Unadorned crystal can be rather more difficult to find as so much of it is used by manufacturers for cut glass or for their own copper wheel engraving. However, if you live in an area where it is not readily available, it is usually a good idea to let your local shop or store know what you need and to ask them to let you know if they receive anything suitable. Another good source of supply can be the sales. Make sure you know when these start and go along early. Bargains in glass are always snapped up at once. Most large stores have a good selection of 'seconds' at sale times and if you choose carefully, it is often very difficult to tell the difference between seconds and first quality – even glass sold as perfect is seldom absolutely free from some irregularity if it is handmade. Antique shops are another good source of supply. By this, I do not mean shops selling expensive antiques but rather those which sell interesting glass at reasonable prices and not necessarily very old. In such places you may perhaps find a single crystal goblet, or one or two wineglasses left over from a set. It is only a personal feeling on my part, but I should be very reluctant, myself, to engrave on genuine antique glass. If I think about it, I suppose there are two reasons for this. One is that I think the period of both the glass and the engraving should be the same; the other is that I think if something as fragile as a piece of glass has miraculously survived down the years it deserves to stand alone and in its own right.

When selecting glass there are a few points to watch for – so do not hurry over your purchase because in doing so you may overlook some faults. It may sound obvious to say 'look for small faults', but many shops and stores have rather inadequate lighting and it is easy to miss something which would not matter to an ordinary customer but which would matter very much to you as an engraver. First, look for small air bubbles. These are are a common occurrence in all handmade glass and you must be prepared to accept one, or a few, provided they are not in a place which would either be very noticeable or which would interfere with your engraving. Next, hold the glass up to a very good light and see if there are any tiny hair lines running round it. It is best for an engraver to avoid these as they may develop into cracks. Then look carefully at the rims of glasses or edges of vases as these are sometimes badly finished and may be slightly wavy. Also, run a finger round the foot and rim of glass as it is not always possible to detect tiny chips or imperfections simply by looking. You will soon learn what are the essential things to look for.

One important point to consider is the amount of space there is which can be engraved. Some glasses have quite a large area at the base which cannot be used. This may be an intentional deep base, or it may simply be a large area of distortion where the glass has naturally thickened towards the base. Sometimes a glass which at first glance appears rather large may prove to have a surprisingly small engravable area.

The foregoing has dealt only with glass shapes of various kinds, but it is possible, of course, to engrave upon flat pieces of glass. You may wish to do this in the beginning for practice, or you may find it useful to have a piece of flat glass available for use as a kind of scribbling pad upon which to try out part of a design. There are two types of flat glass available: one, the thinner of the two, is that used for most domestic windows, for glazing pictures, or in other ways in which inexpensive glass is needed. It is rather hard and should never be used in conjunction with a good diamond hand tool or with new diamond dental burrs. Use carborundum burrs instead or worn diamond burrs. (It is also possible to engrave on the more expensive non-reflective picture glass.) The other kind of flat glass is float glass. This is thicker, costs more and has greater clarity. Indeed, it can look rather handsome if you have the edges rounded off; this is much cheaper than having them bevelled and is very satisfactory. Always explain that you need the glass for engraving so that when it is being cut to your measurements extra care can be taken to ensure that it is absolutely free from scratches.

Working Conditions

Good and comfortable conditions are essential for whatever method of engraving you use, although these need not be elaborate. For instance, you *must* be able to see your work well; you should work in a comfortable position; and you should consider a few common-sense precautions concerning safety.

SEEING YOUR WORK

The amount and type of lighting you need is entirely an individual choice. Some people prefer daylight – even sunlight – though I do feel that in England, at least, this latter requirement must be rather limiting! To a large extent I suppose it is really a question of how fortunate you are in the quality of your eyesight. However, try to avoid working under any sense of strain as far as seeing is concerned. You cannot hope to do satisfying work if you cannot really see what you are doing. A central overhead light in a room is the kind of illumination least likely to give you sufficient light and in the direction in which you need it. So experiment with a small reading lamp until you find the best position for it. Best of all is the kind of lighting which can be obtained from an anglepoise lamp or something similarly adjustable. This can be moved and twisted into any position, height or angle, whenever your work requires it.

POSTURE

This seems to be unimportant to most people so if you are one of the lucky ones, ignore the rest of this paragraph. However, I speak (with *feeling*!) for myself and others like me. Engraving, as I hope you will soon discover, is utterly absorbing and, without realising it, you may find yourself sitting at your work for a considerable time without varying your posture. So first make sure that your work-surface (whether table, cushion on your knees, or whatever else you have chosen) is at the right height and that your shoulders are neither hunched up because it is too low, nor permanently raised because it is too high. It is all too easy to do either of these things. If you are using a flexible drive drill with a foot control, you may find that because one foot, and therefore leg and hip, is slightly raised for long periods of time your back suffers some discomfort. One way to avoid this is to have a support for *both* feet at the same level as the foot control. Some people find they need an arm support when using a Burgess Engraver, particularly the Professional model which is no lightweight. If your forearm as well as your hand is well supported, you will find that the work is easy. Finally, carried away (as I am sure you will be) by the interest of the work and the intensity of your involvement with it, do not grip the glass too tightly! This is all too easy to do. It is no help to the engraving and if you are working on something small and hold it very tightly for rather a long time you will get pretty stiff muscles.

Fortunately, must people notice none of these things so do not let me put you off!

WORKING SAFELY

Surely this is just commonsense, but perhaps I should put a few ideas into your mind.

There is no reason at all why engraving should not be perfectly safe work. You are not, as for example you would be doing all the time if you were working on stained glass, going to *cut* glass at all. You will deal with glass vessels – complete shapes without edges which, themselves, could cut you. You should not grip the glass tightly when working, therefore it should be in no danger of breaking. Nor will you be attacking it violently with mechanical tools. All your work will be gentle so your glass should not be subjected to rough treatment. If for any reason you do break a glass (perhaps merely by dropping it, or, as I have done, by dropping a tool upon it) then you would obviously deal with the broken pieces as you would with any other broken glass. But regard for your work will automatically make you careful about the way in which you handle your glass.

However, there are a few sensible measures to take. One concerns work done on pieces of flat glass. If you are working on float glass for panels or mirrors and you have had the edges rounded off, you will have nothing to worry about. But if you are working on ordinary window glass, or if you have not had the edges of the float glass rounded, it is essential before starting work to protect yourself in some way from the sharp edges of the glass. This can conveniently be done by covering them with passe-partout or masking tape. Use enough layers of either to give an adequately thick covering which will ensure that the edges of the piece of glass do not break through as you handle it.

If you already wear spectacles you automatically have some eye protection, which most people consider adequate. If you do not, you might like to wear some: if you do decide to do this, it is worth deciding whether or not you would find it useful to get some kind of magnification at the same time. Magnifying spectacles are available at most opticians – mounted conveniently on a headband and possible to wear over your own spectacles if necessary.

At all times avoid touching your eyes with your hands. It is in this way that tiny particles of glass could be accidentally deposited in an eye. Glass particles should be especially considered when working with a drill because this can cause a very fine glass 'dust' – whereas

31

PLATES

Plate 1   Tazza, with applied blue threads and diamond engraving. Venetian. First half of seventeenth century *Crown Copyright. Victoria and Albert Museum*

Plate 2   English glass, diamond engraved 1580 *Crown Copyright. Victoria and Albert Museum*

Plate 3   Wineglass with diamond point line engraving, English. Probably made in the glasshouse of G. Verzelini. Dated 1581 *Crown Copyright. Victoria and Albert Museum*

Plate 4   Roemer drinking-glass made of light green glass with raspberry prunts, and diamond engraving of the arms of William III of Orange and seven provinces of the Dutch Republic. German or Dutch glass, mid-seventeenth century *Crown Copyright. Victoria and Albert Museum*

Plate 5   Calligraphic goblets engraved by Willem van Heemskerk (*left* 1680, *right* 1682) *Stedelijk Museum 'de Lakenhal', Leiden (A. Dingjan, The Hague)*

Plate 6   Wineglass, probably English, with stipple engraving by David Wolff, c1786 *Crown Copyright. Victoria and Albert Museum*

Plate 7   Diamond point line engraving on Venetian dish, second half of sixteenth century *Crown Copyright. Victoria and Albert Museum*

Plate 8   Diamond point stipple and drill engraving of Harlech Castle. Eric Smith

Plate 9   Stipple engraving by Peter David using a tungsten carbide tip

Plate 10   Stipple and drill engraving by Barbara Norman

Plate 11   Some typical engraving tools

Plate 12   Deroter flexible drive drill and bench support

Plate 13   Abstract design by Elly Eliades, inspired by sunlight and shade on the roofs of Greek town, Sandorini. Drill engraved and polished

Plate 14   Some useful-size diamond burrs and wheels (actual size)

Plate 15   Selection of carborundum burrs and wheels (actual size)

Plate 16   Engraving by Anne Cotton, using a drill on both the top and under surfaces of a bowl

Plate 17   Polishing tools (actual size). The two on the left are felt tips; the others are rubber and carborundum

Plate 18   Drill engraving of a Florida house by Barbara Norman

Plate 19   Champagne glass matted out with white carborundum burr, engraved with diamond-impregnated wheels and partly polished. By Elly Eliades

Plate 20   Intaglio engraving using dental and flexible drive drill with carborundum and diamond wheels. Polished to produce additional tonal values. *The Mummers* engraved by Jo Birrell *(Colin Hughes)*

I

2

3

4

5

7

8

9

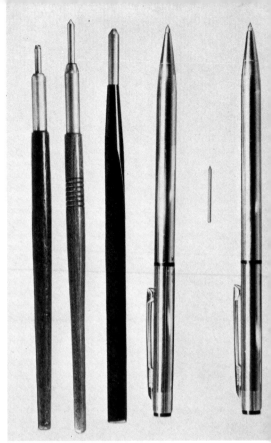

11

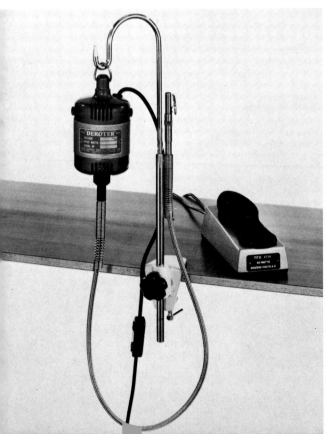

12

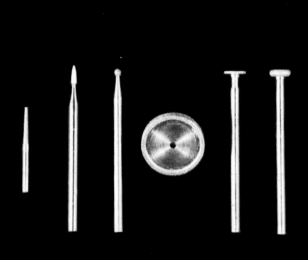

14

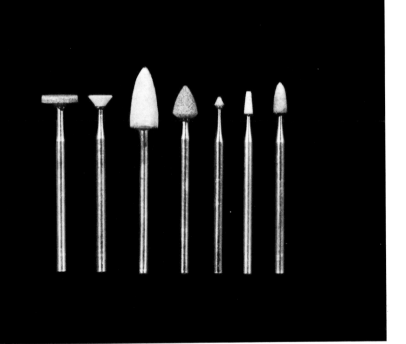

15

16

17

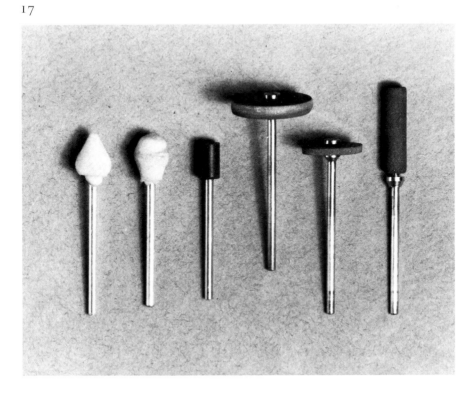

19

diamond point work should only result in some tiny fragments of glass which collect on the glass as you work. So when working with a drill it is sensible to wear some kind of simple mask. Many craft shops supply various grades of masks so choose one which gives the necessary degree of protection. If in doubt, consult the manufacturers and explain the type of work you do.

Finally, a word about electrical tools. Always make sure that these are properly earthed and have the lowest amperage fuse which is practicable. If in doubt consult an expert. Later on, I shall describe some ways in which it is advantageous to work with water. When doing this in the proper way the water does not come into contact with electricity, so always ensure that you observe this. However, if you wish to take the maximum care you may wear shoes with rubber soles or have your work on a rubber mat which your hand touches. If you have any doubts at all about using your chosen tool with water, consult the manufacturer.

WORK SURFACE
If you find you want to raise your work slightly, it is a good idea to place it on a small cushion. This gives some protection to the glass as it avoids any jarring while you are working.

A suitably dark background is essential. Most people work with a small piece of black velvet either behind the glass or inside it. An alternative is any soft, matt black fabric.

Methods of Work

For your first work, try to obtain a glass which does not have a round or curved bowl. Curves are always more difficult to work on and they can distort the design. When you are more experienced you can overcome this but it is more encouraging to choose an easier shape right at the start.

CHOOSING A DESIGN
In order to enjoy the work, the design should, if possible, always be something which you like, but for your first piece of work try to find something simple as this will avoid discouragement. Also, if possible, choose something which harmonises with the shape of the glass. Curved, flowing lines are easier to do than straight ones and

angles. Perhaps you might use some simple combination of flower and leaves, or contrasting leaves by themselves. Try also to find a design which will look well when engraved by your chosen method of work.

A WORKING DRAWING

If you feel you can make a drawing, or even a rough plan, of your intended design, this can be a great help as it provides an opportunity to work out how you are going to deal with light and dark, and it will accustom you to thinking of lightening the light areas instead of 'shading' the dark ones. Many experienced engravers always make drawings first; some prefer to draw straight on to the glass. If you do such a preliminary drawing, you will find it helpful to use a white pencil on black paper (not a *wax* pencil – these are too greasy for working on paper). Working your ideas out first on paper in this way will make you think about tones and which of the light areas is the lightest. Unlike a pencil drawing, you cannot correct an engraving by erasing it and starting again, so if you make any part of it too light it has to remain like that.

MEASURING

In the early stages of your work there will probably not be much need for measuring, except to see that the design is well placed upon the glass and that if it is the sort of thing which has to be straight then it really *is* straight. First of all, you will notice that the increased

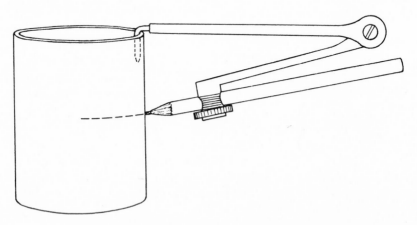

Drawing a line round a glass by means of a compass

thickness which is at the base of all glasses can cause some area of distortion. This can vary with each shape of glass so look carefully at the one you are to work on and decide how far up the glass this distortion shows; sometimes it can become part of the design, for instance if you want the appearance of water. Next, allow about 13mm (½in) between the rim of the glass and the top limit of the design. This is not only because engravings usually look better placed if they do not reach the top of the glass, but also because in some glasses there is an area of stress about 13mm (½in) below the rim and if you engrave at about this level the glass could crack. This stress can be caused by the fact that in the finishing process edges of glasses are heat-treated after the glass has been annealed. The edges then cool in different conditions and at a different rate from the rest of the glass. To engrave an edging design above this level often does not seem to be so hazardous. So, allowing for distortion at the base and avoiding the top 13mm (½in), will give you the area inside which you can do your engraving. You can now work out your design to fit comfortably within these limits.

At some stage you may want to draw guide lines round a glass (useful for placing lettering). There are two easy ways of doing this. One is to bend the point of a simple pair of compasses inwards (you will have to heat it). Then you can simply hang the compasses from the rim of the glass and, using a wax pencil, place lines where you wish. Another method is to turn the glass upside down. Now, hold a wax pencil (or anything else suitable for writing on glass) very firmly against the glass, having your hand supported at the required height. (The support could be a pile of books.) Keep the pencil firm and steady and rotate the glass against it. Vertical lines can be marked on a glass by means of a simple plumbline. Tie a small weight to the end of a piece of thick thread. Attach the other end to the top of the glass by means of a piece of sellotape (scotch tape) so that the thread and weight hang down. Then put a series of small marks on the glass along the line of the thread by means of a wax pencil.

PUTTING THE DESIGN ON THE GLASS

There are several ways of putting a design on a glass in readiness for engraving. It is really a matter of personal choice and the same methods can be used for all the different methods of engraving. All are very simple and require very little equipment.

51

By Drawing

There are several methods of drawing or painting directly on to the glass. Whether you choose to draw or to paint depends solely upon whether you feel you can work better with a pencil or a brush. Some people feel they can produce more easily flowing lines with one than the other. First, drawing with a pencil. For this you will need a wax pencil or any of the various types of pencil available for marking on glass or plastic. The colour is important: it should be either light or bright. White, yellow, pale blue, light red – all these are good to work with as they show up well against a black velvet background in all conditions of light. Some types of pencil will only work well on glass that has been well handled and therefore has a slight coating of grease from your hand on it. Others will only make marks on glass which is absolutely clean and free from any trace of grease. So either handle the glass well or wash it, as necessary.

Having chosen a pencil and prepared the surface of the glass, draw on the design and correct mistakes by rubbing off with a finger. Keep the pencil lines as thin as possible; thick lines get in the way of engraving and are a nuisance to clean off.

It is also possible to draw directly on to glass with a Staedtler Lumocolor Permanent. This is spirit based and once it is dry, you must use acetone (nail polish remover) to clean it off, so corrections in drawing should be made before it dries.

By Painting

If you prefer to work with a brush you will find it easy to paint on glass. To do this you need a fine water-colour brush (there is no need to get an expensive one). For paint you can use either process white or poster paint in whatever colour you like – but, as with pencils, light or bright paint is best. Simply mix the paint with a little water (do not make it too runny) and paint your design on to the glass. When the paint has dried completely you can fine down any lines which are too thick simply by scraping away any surplus paint with an orange stick or cocktail stick. Some paintbrushes even have ends which are sharp enough to be used for this purpose.

A more permanent painting can be obtained if you mix the paint with thin liquid water-soluble glue instead of water.

By Poster Paint and Lead Pencil

If you find you can draw on glass with a pencil more easily than you can paint, you might like to try a method which is a combination of both. Use *coloured* poster paint this time (not white), instead of water, moisten with water-soluble liquid glue, and paint this evenly over a large enough area of glass to take your design. Allow the paint to dry thoroughly and then draw on your design with a very soft lead pencil (at least 2B). A soft lead is important, particularly if you are working on lead crystal as a hard lead could scratch the glass. This method of drawing over paint has the advantage that the pencil drawing may be corrected by using a *very* soft eraser. The combination of painting and drawing shows up well when you engrave it if you arrange for light to shine directly into or through the glass rather than down on to it. As you engrave you will realise that had you used white paint in this instance the engraving would not show up against it as you progress.

By Tracing

If you feel unable to draw a design on to glass it is just as easy to trace it. In fact, if you have already made a working drawing you may, in any case, now want to trace from your own drawing.

The first requirement is, ideally, tracing paper. Failing that, greaseproof paper will do. (NB for the USA: *not* waxed paper.) Masking tape is also very useful as it enables you to fix your piece of tracing paper over the design you want to trace without damaging the paper upon which the design appears.

So, cut a piece of tracing paper to a suitable size, tape it down (if possible) over the design and trace the design with a sharp-pointed pencil. HB is good (but keep the point sharpened) or something a little harder. If you use anything too hard you will end up with a very faint tracing and may also damage the page from which you are making the tracing. If necessary, mark on the tracing paper the top and bottom of an imaginary vertical line through the design, or any other useful guide marks, so that you can place the tracing correctly on the glass. Now, on the back of the tracing, scribble all over the traced design with a wax pencil. Make sure that you do this evenly and that you have completely covered the design. Do not produce too thick a coating of wax pencil or, at the next stage, you will end up with a smudged outline on the glass.

53

If you have made guide marks (for example, for the vertical) on the tracing paper, make them also on the glass (see page 51). Now, with sellotape (scotch tape) or masking tape, fix the traced design to the glass, matching the guide marks. The final stage is to trace over the design again with something hard and sharp. This could be a *fine*-tip ballpoint pen or a 6H pencil with a very sharp point or anything else which, although sharp, will not cut through the tracing paper. Before you remove the piece of tracing paper from the glass, hold the glass near a light at such an angle that you can see from the inside whether or not you have *completely* traced the design. If you get the light through the glass at the right angle it is possible to see this – it is a great disappointment to find, when you remove the tracing paper, that you have left out even a tiny part of the design. You should now have a clear imprint of the design upon the glass, but if you want to strengthen this you can go over it with a fine mapping pen (or Rotring pen with a fine nib) and Rotring waterproof ink. Black is a good colour for this.

Using Carbon Paper

Many people prefer to use carbon paper at the back of a tracing instead of using the scribbling method. If you choose this method, all you need is ordinary carbon paper as used for typing. Try to get a kind that will produce the thinnest lines when you use it for tracing. One extremely good kind which does not smudge and which produces *very* fine lines is that used in dressmaking and this can be bought in packets from shops selling sewing aids. The packets usually contain large sheets of paper in various colours – probably white, orange and dark blue or purple. All are useful, though if you use the blue or purple you will probably have to work against some other background than black velvet.

The first part of the method is as described above – ie place a piece of tracing paper over your design and make a pencil tracing of it. Now cut off a piece of carbon paper to fit the tracing. Tape the tracing paper and the piece of carbon paper securely to the glass, with the carbon side next to the glass. Trace over the design as in the previous method. When you remove the tracing you should have your outline traced on to the glass.

Prevention of Smudging

In some of the above methods you may wish to protect the design for smudging while you are working on it. There are two ways of doing this: Cling Film (Glad Wrap) or some kind of spray fixative. The latter can be hairspray or pastel fixative. The advantage of the film is that you can move it around as you work and there is nothing to clean off the glass afterwards.

Using a Photograph or Drawing

Some engravers find it satisfactory and easy to place their working drawing (or a photograph or other printed illustration) behind or inside the glass and to work directly from that. The illustration must be fixed firmly in position by means of adhesive tape. However, according to the thickness of the glass, there can be a certain amount of distortion – like looking at an object through water. It is essential to look directly down on to the glass so that you do not see the design at an angle. If you use this method, one helpful visual aid is to coat the required area of glass on the outside with a spirit-based transparent marker (red is a good colour). This shows up the engraving against the photograph as you work, and you can see exactly where you are.

Types of Engraving

Probably one of the greatest difficulties for a new engraver is the lack of opportunity to *see* exactly what it is all about. It is all very well to feel that here is a craft which is new to you and at which you would like to work, but it can be very daunting at first to have to embark on it without ever having seen any actual work. Now, suppose you have put a design on a glass, what exactly are you aiming for? Just what kind of work will each tool accomplish? For this reason, and because so many people have not yet had an opportunity to see hand-engraved glass, I give rather detailed descriptions of the appearance of each kind of work. It is also hoped that the many photographs in this book will help to show the great range of work and design that can be achieved, and will help you to take the first steps. Of course, many people live in areas some distance from museums and galleries, but the strange thing is that, once you have become interested in engraving, you suddenly seem to keep hearing about it. You notice mention of it in newspapers and magazines, sometimes quite lengthy articles about it. You see photographs of it; you hear of someone's work being exhibited in a nearby gallery of whose existence you might previously have been unaware. Sometimes there are television programmes about it. You may find a few pieces in quite unexpected shops. I have found that I receive a constant flow of information from friends about all kinds of things connected with glass and engraving. Once your own enthusiasm is known, people are eager to pass on anything of interest which comes their way.

Diamond Point Engraving

Diamond point engraving, done with a diamond tool held in your hand, is the oldest form of engraving and was in use before the more mechanised wheel engraving. It can be done with a variety of tools – which will be listed and described later – on all types of glass, though the technique used depends to a great extent upon the type of glass.

The two methods used in diamond point engraving are lines and tiny stippled dots. What you are aiming for when using only lines is to arrange them in such a way, in varying directions, that you build up an interesting design. Sometimes you will want to create an entirely matt white effect and this can be done by placing the lines very close together, perhaps cross-hatching them, and, finally, gently scratching the surface until it is matted over. How deeply should the lines be cut into the glass? Deep enough to be clearly visible but they should not be drawn by using the tool with great pressure. If you run a finger over the finished work you should be able to feel a light scratching on the surface of the glass. Plates 1 and 2 show the interesting and very satisfying way in which engravers in past centuries worked with lines alone. Designs engraved by lines have quite a strong appearance and the design is easily visible in all but the poorest light. This method, therefore, is well suited for use on anything that is to be *used* as it does not need special illumination or display. Naturally, though, you may have chosen to do a line engraving on something that is only for display.

The second method used in diamond point engraving, stipple, consists of working entirely by dots placed very close together. It sounds as if it must surely be a very slow method of work but it is not. Stippling is done at speed – in fact it is difficult to do it slowly and still maintain an even flow of dots. When the dots are placed very close together and the diamond tool taps the glass with increased pressure, the result is denser and whiter. The whiteness is 'faded out' (thus producing a darkening effect) by using the tool more lightly. How deeply should the dots penetrate the surface of the glass and how hard should you tap with the diamond tool? Fine stipple engraving is almost impossible to feel when passing a fingertip over the glass. To achieve this, and to deal kindly with your precious tool, means that the tapping must be delicate.

I always think that diamond point stipple engraving produces the real magic of engraving. At its most delicate it can be scarcely visible on a glass. Yet, turn the glass to catch the light, and suddenly there is a picture on it. It is mysterious and fugitive. Of course, not all stipple engraving is – or need be – as delicate as that; quite strong effects can be obtained if you wish. Yet always there is this slightly luminous air about it, a faint sheen. I think this is probably because as each tiny dot is made, the surface of the glass is cut by the very fine, sharp diamond and thus each dot reflects some light. Stipple engraving has quite a different appearance from matt areas produced by using lines.

If you are doing a piece of stipple engraving at someone's request it is often helpful to both you and the other person if you can find out if they are accustomed to seeing this kind of work. If you are planning to do very delicate stipple engraving, it would be wise to ask if this is what is really expected, because it should be displayed with special lighting if full justice is to be done to your work. Simply put on a shelf, engraving such as this can be almost invisible – the magic is entirely lost – and it can be a disappointment to the recipient. But with the right lighting (as described in Chapter 4) the engraving is transformed into something ethereal. So if it is not intended to display such delicate work with suitable illumination, it would be better to consider using stipple in a stronger way in order to produce a more visible result.

Mixing Lines and Stipple
There may be some occasions when you will want to mix both methods. For example, it is sometimes effective to use lines for the stamens of flowers which, themselves, have been engraved by the stipple method. You will discover more possibilities for this mixing of methods as you work on and get more ideas about how you want an engraving to look.

57

TOOLS

If you are attracted by the idea of diamond point engraving with a hand tool, you need to know what the tools look like, what different types there are, and what kind of work the different tools are used for. You will find that there are several from which to choose. First, do not be misled by the idea of *diamonds*. Those used in engraving tools are not beautiful, glittering objects, costing a fortune. They are very tiny industrial diamonds and really do not look in the least like the gemstones we all know. I was once allowed to hold a pile of these tiny diamonds in the palm of my hand: it was just like a little heap of rather coarse sand.

The simplest, and cheapest, tool is a tiny 'chip' of diamond set in a wooden holder. The diamond has various natural sharp edges, and when you use this tool it is a good idea to mark it in some way after you have discovered where these edges are so that you can easily know the right position in which to hold it. It can be used very suc-cessfully for linear work and, if the glass on which you are working is soft enough, you can get some interesting stipple effects (although this tool will not produce very delicate stipple). Many people start with this basic tool and use it for working on inexpensive glass. It is a good way to get the feel of working on glass and to get used to the idea of portraying light and dark.

Another tool which is made of a 'chip' of diamond has a somewhat larger diamond which protrudes beyond the end of the tool. This, too, has various cutting edges but they are sharper than those in the basic tool. The fact that the diamond protrudes makes it easier to work with as you can see its exact position on the glass. This tool can be used for stippling.

Then there are those tools in which the diamond is sharpened to a precise angle, as in the Lunzer Lancer. This angle can be 90°, 75° or 60°. These tools are really like marvellous precision instruments and need careful use. A common error beginners make is to think that diamonds are extremely hard and absolutely indestructible. This is not so at all. They are crystals, and if they are used carelessly or with too much force, they will chip or splinter. Then you will be left with some kind of cutting edge but no longer with the needle-fine point with which you started. However, there is not the slightest need to use a diamond tool other than very gently because if you are using it for drawing lines, you won't want to carve deep furrows, and if you are stippling tiny dots with it, you will only achieve fine delicate results by using it gently. So, with proper use, a Lancer tool has a long life.

An alternative to diamond tools are those made of tungsten carbide. These can be either small 'needles' of tungsten carbide mounted in holders, or separate tips. In the latter case, you buy a holder and replace the tips as they become blunt. When they are very sharp, tungsten carbide tips can produce extremely fine stipple engraving, but they do need frequent sharpening. A drill, or some similar piece of equipment, is essential in sharpening tungsten carbide tips used either in hand tools or in a Burgess Engraver. One method of doing this is to rotate a diamond disc or wheel in the drill and hold the tungsten carbide tip against it.

It is a matter of personal choice whether you prefer diamond or tungsten carbide tools. (Incidentally, if you work with tungsten carbide tips your work could be described as 'point engraving'.) I myself confess to a preference for diamonds. Diamonds last very much longer and some kinds can be resharpened by the makers. In any case, you can almost always find *some* use for a diamond which is past its best.

As your choice of tools may have to be made on the basis of descriptions or photographs, a general example of some of the various tools available is shown in plate 11. From left to right these are.

(1) Simple 'writing diamond' (a tiny natural diamond chip).
(2) Small sharpened diamond tip.
(3) Larger natural diamond chip, unsharpened.
(4) Lunzer Lancer engraving tool with diamond sharpened to 90° point.
(5) Unmounted tungsten carbide tip for use in clutch holder.
(6) Lunzer Lancer with tungsten carbide tip.

Price

It is not practicable to give prices of tools as these could change. But some guide can at least be given as regards diamond hand tools. The cheapest ones can be compared with a modest ballpoint pen (*not* the very cheap, throwaway kind, of course!) A tool with a point sharpened to a stated angle (Lunzer Lancer) would cost about the same as a good ballpoint pen. When considering electrical tools, flexible drive drills are much more expensive than diamond hand tools but they open up a very wide range of work, and for anyone prepared to invest in mechanical equipment they are an endless source of interest and experiment.

WORKING ON FLAT GLASS

First, see whether or not you would enjoy engraving by trying it out on a flat piece of glass, using the simplest tool. If possible use float glass (commonly known as plate glass) rather than window glass. It costs a little more but is infinitely better to work on, and you can even practise stippling on it. If you cannot afford more than ordinary window glass, then only use the basic tool. You should not expect miracles from window glass, but it can at least provide good practice in the various ways of putting a design on to glass. As the various kinds of equipment needed for this practice work are inexpensive, you may feel able to try several methods of engraving. Flat glass can also give you a good idea of what it is like to put your design behind glass and engrave straight from this without any drawing or tracing. It will also give you an opportunity to find the best cutting edges on your tool and you can as previously suggested, mark the handle so that you know in future which way round to hold it. Although you cannot do fine stipple engraving on ordinary window glass, you can at least discover the speed at which you can do the stippling. As for designs for this first practice, try something simple like some leaves or grasses, or a pattern or geometrical shapes – something which will provide an opportunity to use lines or rather coarse stippling in an interesting way. This will not put much strain on your tool and you will get accustomed to thinking in terms of black and white. (Stipple engraving itself is dealt with on page 61).

Put the design on to the glass, using one of the methods described on pages 52–5. Draw the outline of the design with the diamond tool. Continue working with lines (or coarse stippling) as if you were using a pencil. The only difference is that you will be working at the light areas and lightening them, not shading in the dark areas.

WORKING ON A GLASS
Using Lines

If you have chosen a piece of soda glass you could plan, as your first work, a design which could be engraved with lines. If you find that the glass is not too hard you might, for practice, be able to incorporate some stipple too. The simplest tool could be used for this.

Using Stipple

Stipple engraving can be used for a tremendous range of subjects, as can be seen from many photographs in this book. The most delicate contrasts of tone can be achieved. A subject may be very fully engraved or a whole scene may be captured by means of a very small amount of engraving. Sometimes the foreground may be dark and the background light, as in 'Windmill' by Eric Smith (illustrated in plate 47). Photographs of many styles of stipple engraving have been included in this book, both old and new, so that many different approaches to subjects may be seen.

Try to work on the best glass you can afford if you want to do stipple engraving, and use a good tool – either diamond or tungsten carbide. You might start with a diamond tool with a 90° point (a Lunzer Lancer) which will give quite fine stippling. If you use a Lunzer tool you can buy refills for less than the cost of a complete tool so you might, later on, be able to add to your collection of tools by buying refills with finer points such as 75° or 60° both of which can produce very fine stipple.

By looking at the photographs you can see the different ways in which the engravers have interpreted their subjects, and this should help in your own decisions on how you will deal with your chosen design. Even if you do not do a preliminary drawing, it is essential to work out in your mind exactly how you wish to portray the subject before you start work. Decide which is the lightest part and where the deepest shadow is. It is important to decide where there are half-tones because if you make a mistake when fading out the strength of your stippling, it is not usually possible to do much about modifying the rest of the work.

Having drawn or traced the design on to the glass, the way you deal with the outline when working by stipple is really an individual matter. Some engravers with a very steady touch simply make a few faint marks to denote the outline and are able to stipple the rest at speed without further help. Others find they have to indicate the whole outline by carefully, and more slowly, placing dots very close together to form a continuous line. Only practice will show you which method is for you.

When stippling the design itself, try to get the dots placed sufficiently close together the first time as it is not satisfactory to have to go over an area of engraving a second time.

You can, if you wish, just sharpen a line where necessary by gently drawing a very fine diamond along the outline.

Combining Stipple and Drill

A much more positive effect can be achieved if a drill is used in conjunction with stipple. This combined method does not mean the work is inferior – like painting, engraving can be anything you want it to be as long as it is well done and interprets a subject successfully. Delicate stipple engraving may not be to everyone's taste and, as has already been said, it really does require special conditions for display. So, if you have a drill, you can use it to give a whiter matt effect where you need this and to give bolder lines and clear outlines. The type of burr you use is, as always, a matter of choice, but it is likely that a fine diamond burr will give the boldest, sharpest results.

WORKING WITH TUNGSTEN CARBIDE TOOLS

Many engravers use tungsten carbide tools and many prefer them. It is certainly true, I think, that a very sharp carbide tool used to stipple on full lead crystal does give a more delicate result. So where this is the effect you need, you might wish to work with this tool. If you use tungsten carbide tips you must be prepared to sharpen them frequently. In some instances, the manufacturers of the separate tips are prepared to sharpen these so it is always worth enquiring the cost of this and the time it is likely to take.

Sharp tungsten carbide tools can be used to draw very fine lines and are therefore useful for lettering. Also, they protrude as far as the point of a sharp pencil and this can be a great help.

Because they produce such delicate stippling when they are sharp these tools can be very useful if you wish to indicate an outline by means of separately placed dots. Used for this purpose, a tungsten carbide tip will give a very faint but clear outline.

Drill Engraving

The next type of engraving is that done with a dental drill or flexible drive drill. Engraving on glass with a drill offers seemingly endless opportunities for inventive work. The great number and variety of dental burrs available all produce different results and as well as engraving glass it is also possible to polish your engraving in various ways and to varying degrees, thus extending still further the range of work that can be done. While not seeking to imitate copper wheel engraving, some work done with a drill can have certain similarities to that done with a wheel, whereas work done with diamond or tungsten carbide hand tools is totally different. Indeed, drill engraving might be said to bridge a gap between diamond point and copper wheel. Drill engraving is, above all, very visible. If done lightly, and perhaps also polished, it does not cut deeply into the glass. However, on thicker glass you can cut into the surface as deeply as you wish and can, indeed, produce sculptured effects in much the same way as those achieved by copper wheel engraving.

All kinds of glass are suitable for drill engraving, although naturally if you are working on anything extremely hard it will take its toll of the burrs. Although it is possible to do quite delicate work with a drill, on the whole it is best not to work on very thin glass. However, drill engraving does make it possible to work on a wider range and quality of glass than you would normally consider when doing diamond point as there is no stippling to worry about.

As for suitable subjects, these are really without limit: interpretation is what matters. Like diamond point stipple engraving, all degrees of tone can be achieved with a drill. Whereas with stipple engraving shadow is achieved by ever more delicate dots, in drill engraving you can use special tips for the drill which will polish out your engraving, thus producing shadow.

As will be shown later on in the chapter, a drill is particularly suitable for lettering.

TOOLS FOR DRILL ENGRAVING

Although worked by a motor, a good drill makes little noise. A typical model is illustrated in plate 12. From this you can see that it consists of an electric motor, a cable and a detachable handpiece. In fact this is a model which is used by dental mechanics and is particularly suited to glass engraving. This particular model has a foot control; other makes have a hand control in the form of a small button on the handpiece which is pressed down with the index finger.

Ideally, the motor should be suspended above your worksurface. This not only gives you far more control over the cable and hand-piece, but also ensures that the cable does not become twisted. If you have a studio in which to work, it might not be a problem to find some place from which to suspend the motor (they are fitted with rings specially for the purpose). However, if you have to work at an ordinary table somewhere about the house, a special metal support (a bench support) is available. If the table is well padded, the support will not mark it.

Now for the burrs. As in the case of diamond hand tools, probably few people have seen many dental burrs – at least not in detail! These are made of either diamond particles or a hard stone (carborundum). Diamond burrs are either coated or impregnated with tiny particles of diamond (the impregnated kind cost more but last much longer). They produce much sharper outlines and give a sharper effect where the glass is matted over. Carborundum burrs, which are made in varying degrees of hardness, do not produce such clean lines and the matted effect which they produce is softer and does not penetrate so deeply into the glass. Diamond burrs should be used for lettering.

To buy these burrs, you should go to a dental supplier and ask to see a catalogue. There you will find actual-size reproductions of the range of burrs. Until you get accustomed to using them and have dis-covered which are best for your kind of work, only buy small quan-tities. Indeed, you may at first want to limit yourself to a single diamond burr and about six carborundum ones. To give you some idea of what is available in the way of burrs, plates 14 and 15 show some typical examples – actual size.

Opinions differ on whether burrs last longer if the drill is run at a fairly high speed or at a slow speed. It is suggested, therefore, that it would be wise to check this with the particular manufacturer from whom you buy your equipment.

It pays to take good care of your drill so make sure you have been provided with information about how to keep it well lubricated.

STARTING WORK

Designs are drawn or traced on to the glass in the ways already described on pages 52–5. However, if you are going to engrave with water (which is explained below) you will not be able to use paint, liquid glue or any kind of ink which would wash off.

If you want to use a piece of window glass for experimenting, do only use an old, worn diamond burr as this glass is far too hard for new diamond burrs. (New diamond burrs can be used with care on float glass.) You can also use up an old carborundum one which will at least give you an idea of how you want to deal with a particular aspect of the subject. First, you could use the drill as if you were drawing with a pencil. Do the outline of the design so that the wax pencil or paint, etc, may be wiped off. Now fill in the design in whatever way you like, changing burrs as necessary.

Working with Water

If you use water in conjunction with a drill this will greatly extend the life of the burrs. *But, as already noted on page 49, great care must be taken to keep all moisture well away from electricity.* In addition, the use of water produces a slightly different appearance in the work – perhaps best described by saying that matted areas seem to look just a little smoother. It also produces much cleaner, sharper outlines.

There are various ways of providing a supply of water. If you have a workshop you will probably be able to arrange things so that you can have a drip supply directly on to your work. (You only need a drip at a time, but steadily.) Of course, you will need something to catch the water because, even drop by drop, the amount adds up after a while. I am indebted to a friend, Majella Taylor, for an ingenious idea for dealing with this. She works with a meat roasting tin and a plastic-covered wire plate-rack! When the rack is placed upside down in the tin it forms a bed for the piece of glass. The water runs down off the glass and into the tin.

If you have to work, say, at your dining table, you will have to make do with something much simpler and a little more trouble to operate. In this case you can use a small eye-dropper, obtainable from a chemist. You just drip water from it on to your work, as required. Slower, of course, but perfectly manageable. If you use an eye-dropper, the work must be wiped frequently as there is no continuous drip to wash away the glass particles which will collect and obscure the work. Another very simple method of working with water is constantly to sponge the glass with water while engraving.

Polishing

Having experimented with the effects produced by various burrs, you may now want to find out how to polish out some of the engraving you have done and discover to what extent it can be done. Of course it is not necessary to polish if you are working with a drill, but the process does add immensely to the range of your work and makes it much more interesting both to look at and to do. It is painstaking work but well worth the time spent on it as it produces effects which can be obtained in no other way.

Polishing can be done in many ways and with quite a variety of special wheels and other aids. Some of these (actual size) are illustrated in plate 17. All, except the felt ones, are bought from dental suppliers. The felt wheels and tips can be bought either at craft shops or from specialists in stone polishing (not gemstones, though).

In conjunction with most of the wheels and tips some kind of fine abrasive powder is necessary. Also, commercial metal polishes such as Brasso and Goddards give good results.

The effect of polishing is to diminish the whiteness caused by grinding the surface of the glass with a diamond or carborundum burr; thus a darker area is created. The more the engraving is polished the less whiteness remains, therefore maximum darkness requires the most polishing. The results can be extremely attractive as the areas which have been polished take on a soft gleam. When polishing, it is important not to press the polisher down hard upon the glass. The length of time it takes to polish depends upon the texture of the tool you are using and the softness of the glass.

The rubber wheels and tips, impregnated with carborundum, polish fairly quickly, but in doing so some of the softer ones wear away moderately quickly. Wheels made of wood or cork should be used with a fine abrasive powder mixed with water or fine-grade oil. (Pumice grade 600 is good.) They take longer to polish but give fine and luminous results. Thick wooden matchsticks give the same results as wooden wheels and are useful for small areas. Felt wheels and other felt shapes should also be used with fine abrasive powder and water. They act gently on the glass and are used as a final process.

Making Your Own Polishing Wheels

These can be made from wood or cork. If you want wooden wheels you can either buy dowel-rod and have it cut into thin slices (say

3mm (¹⁄₁₀in) or just cut slices from the handle of any item of kitchen equipment. Cork wheels are simply slices cut from an ordinary cork. To mount the home-made wheels ready for use in a drill you will need a mandrel (obtainable from a dental supplier or hardware shop).

OTHER USES FOR DRILL ENGRAVING

So far, mention has only been made of using a drill on a piece of flat glass for practice purposes and of working on actual glass. The latter includes, of course, all glass shapes such as vases, decanters, bowls or anything else that is suitable. This method can also be used, however, for engraving decorative panels, tables, mirrors, doors, windows or pictures. All these need a strong effect and a drill is just the right method.

Decorative Panels

These can be of any practicable size if they are to be used as free-standing decoration in a room, and they can be displayed in heavy wooden bases. Such panels are very effective and show up well with light behind them – either daylight or artificial light. It is best to display them with the engraving at the back as when this is viewed through the glass it gains greatly in depth and brilliance. In cases where you wish to introduce extra depth into a subject you can engrave on two – or more – panels and exhibit them one in front of the other as Anne Dybka has done (see plate 21).

An even more effective way is for light to pass straight through the glass. This is a little more difficult to arrange, but it can be done by constructing a wooden box frame which is deep enough from back to front to enclose fluorescent strip lighting. (This is cooler than ordinary electric strip lighting.) Even fluorescent lighting needs plenty of air holes, however, to ensure that it does not overheat. If you are not sure you have sufficient knowledge to deal with the electrical requirements of such frames, it would be best to consult an electrician. Float (plate) glass, 5mm (¼in) thick, is good for glass panels of this kind; the edges should be rounded off.

Tables

Drill engraving can be used for decorating glass-topped tables, and in this case the work should be done on the underside of the glass. As a very visible design is required and as the glass will probably be hard, somewhat larger carborundum burrs are likely to be useful in matting out large areas. These can be obtained from hardware stores, not dental suppliers.

If you are engraving a set of small tables, one very effective way of working out a design for these is to choose something which can be divided between the number of tables in the set. Each table should have a complete design of its own, but when all the tables are placed together their designs should fit so as to make one whole.

Mirrors

These are engraved first and silvered afterwards. Work on 5mm ($\frac{1}{4}$in) float (plate) glass as for panels. Treat the glass with great care while you are working because even the tiniest mark shows up very clearly when the silvering is applied. Try to brush away any glass particles with a soft cloth rather than with your hand. To get the maximum effect from an engraved mirror, choose a subject which has to be rather fully engraved. You can combine drill with lines or stipple done with a diamond hand tool, and you can also polish parts of the drill engraving. Silvering placed over the engraving produces very interesting and attractive results. Everything shows, even quite fine work done with a diamond hand tool. A very important point is always make it clear the silvering must be applied to the *engraved* side of the glass.

When working on tables or mirrors, or on any surface which has the engraving on the underside, you must bear in mind the possible need to reverse the design.

Doors

The photograph of doors at Stapleford Church, engraved by David Peace, shows a fine example of this method of work (see plate 46). Doors are often made of toughened glass, but the advice of the Glass and Glazing Federation is that you should do the engraving first and have the glass toughened afterwards. There are two methods of toughening: vertical and horizontal. In the vertical method clips are used to hold the glass and some marks from these may be left in the glass. Vertical toughening can also sometimes produce distortion in the engraving. The Federation therefore advises horizontal toughening which leaves neither marks nor distortion. There are many firms who toughen glass but if you have difficulty in finding one you may apply to the Federation for information (address in the Appendix).

Windows

In at least one instance, a window has been a great beginning, as Laurence Whistler relates in his book. *The Image on the Glass.* When this particular window was engraved it was a rare event. Now, however, with the advent of so much drill engraving much more of this sort of work is being done, and not only in churches.

It can be physically demanding as in many cases the window is already in position and the engraver has to climb about on scaffolding to get to the work. Lighting is also different as you work with varying amounts of daylight behind your engraving. If the window is not already in position, special frames often have to be constructed to support the glass.

Some of the best known windows are those done by John Hutton for Coventry Cathedral. There are ninety of these and the work took ten years to complete. Fortunately, more of John Hutton's wonderful work can be seen in other parts of the world. For such large windows he used a hand drill with very large carborundum wheels, and worked with water.

Pictures

These are most effective if they are kept to a small size and engraved miniatures can look very attractive.

The subject should be something which can be portrayed in strong contrasts of light and dark as, in this case, half-tones do not show up very well. The engravings should be mounted against a matt black background or some other very dark matt background. If using velvet this should have a short pile; expensive velvet with a silky pile squashes down with a rather visible sheen when pressed against the glass.

The engraving should be done on the underside of the glass. Another method, if the frame will accommodate the thickness, is to use two pieces of glass and engrave on the front of the inside piece, placing the other piece over it. By doing this there is no need to reverse a subject if you need it to be a particular way round. If you want a greater illusion of depth, you can engrave on the underneath surfaces of two pieces of glass, provided the subject is suitable for division in this way.

Glass 'Rocks' or Cullets

It is sometimes possible to buy a cullet. In the real sense, this is a rough chunk of glass which has been broken out of the deposit left at the bottom of an old pot. It has many surfaces and angles, some of which may be suitable for engraving. However, some glass manu-facturers make mould-blown cullets of crystal which are perfectly polished. These, too, have many surfaces and angles and, some-times, bubbles or quite large irregularities inside the glass. They are a great challenge to an engraver and can be very effective when engraved. The interesting part of working on cullets is trying to use the various surfaces so that they form part of one whole. Sometimes it is possible to use them in such a way that they create reflections.

The Burgess Engraver

Another means of engraving with an electric tool is to use a Burgess Engraver. This tool is totally different from a drill and produces very different work. It is capable of giving a wide range of effects and some engravers use nothing else. The technical definition of the engraver is an electric non-rotary vibrating tool, and the engraving is done by vibrating various sharp points on the surface of the glass.

There are two models of Burgess Engraver. One, the lighter in weight, is the Hobbyist. This is provided with some points suitable for working on glass as well as several other attachments for work on other materials. It has a control dial which varies the stroke.

The Professional model gives a better performance because it has more weight, more positive stroke adjustment and can be used con-tinuously. One additional great advantage is that it is much less noisy than the Hobbyist model and, when adjusted for delicate work, it is barely audible.

A Burgess Professional Engraver can be used for linear work, stip-pling and general matting over of the surface of the glass. According to the adjustment you make to the tool, it can produce very delicate stippling or quite a heavy effect. Lines, too, can be made to vary in intensity. Practice is needed before you discover the wide range of work that the tool can do. Some effects can be produced very quickly

– for example, if you use the tool to write directly on to the glass or to do the equivalent of quick pen and ink sketches. An example of the type of work achieved is illustrated in plate 41. A great advantage of the Engraver is that all the various points protrude well beyond the collet and their exact position on the glass can be clearly seen. The standard points supplied include a special long tungsten carbide tip, reference no A2, which fits into the standard collet. When necessary, the makers of Burgess tools will supply the names of stockists (see Appendix). Like all tungsten carbide points these need fairly frequent sharpening. Unlike the tips for use in hand tools, they may be sharpened satisfactorily by hand – rotating the point firmly along a hard sharpening stone – or, much more speedily, by holding it against a green grit wheel attached to an electric drill which is, in turn, held in a horizontal stand. It is convenient, while doing this, to leave the point in the Engraver.

In addition to long tungsten carbide points, a diamond point is now available, reference no 700066. This, of course, is not suitable for sharpening.

It is also possible to get varied effects with a Burgess Engraver by using various dental burrs, both diamond and carborundum (although some of these may necessitate a different collet). This gives you an opportunity to use diamond burrs that are slightly worn, which will give some interesting stippled effects when used in a Burgess tool.

Lettering

Some people have such a happy aptitude for lettering that they prefer to engrave little else. Others find it more difficult, but there must be few who do not sometimes want to incorporate it into designs.

TOOLS
Lettering can be done with any kind of engraving tool – a diamond or tungsten carbide hand tool, a flexible drive drill or a Burgess Engraver.

If you are using a hand tool the work is made much easier if you choose one where the diamond protrudes well beyond the end of the holders so that you can see exactly where it touches the glass. This is no problem with a tungsten carbide tool – the tip always protrudes.

71

GLASS

Although you can work on any kind of glass, some kinds of soda glass splinter very slightly and this makes it impossible to get clean edges to the letters. Glass with a very curved surface is more difficult to work on than something with straight sides, particularly if you are tracing the letters.

PLANNING THE WORK

The first question is whether the lettering is to be an addition to a design (for example, initials), or whether it is to form a design in itself. (See plates 5 and 29 for examples of the latter.)

If you cannot rise to such heights then there is a great range of lettering from which to choose. Many successful professional engravers have to work directly from printed lettering – their skill in designing the layout and in executing the work is what matters. If you decide to use printed lettering, there are many inexpensive books available which give examples of printed alphabets and some which give examples of calligraphic handwriting. Another good source of ready-made alphabets is Letraset (see below), which is available in a great variety of styles.

PLACING LETTERS ON GLASS

This can be done by all the usual tracing methods or, if you prefer, you can draw or paint directly on to the glass. If the printed alphabet you have chosen is the wrong size and needs redrawing before you can trace it, you may find it helpful to do this on graph paper.

There are two ways of using Letraset. You can either put it straight on to the glass and engrave from that, or you can first put it on to paper and trace it. If you put it straight on to the glass, you must fix it in some way as it peels off when touched with an engraving tool. A fixative could be hairspray, pastel fixative, or one made by Letraset.

METHODS OF WORK

The best advice is to say – use the method you find easiest. Lettering requires practice. If you are using a diamond or tungsten carbide tool, you can draw the outline of the letters very lightly and then fill them in by scratching or cross-hatching. Or you can start by drawing a faint centre line and working gradually outwards with your filling process.

If you are using a drill, choose a diamond burr which has a fine point and gives a clean edge. Many people find it helpful to keep turning the work, easing the point of the burr round curves and always doing straight lines in one direction.

Acid Etching

I am including some reference to acid etching because, in certain circumstances, it can be used successfully in conjunction with engraving.

It is really an industrial process, needing a strong chemical (hydrofluoric acid) which eats into the surface of the glass. However, it is possible to buy an etching cream (Etchall – for supplier see page 182). This is sold in tubes and is for use at home on small areas of glass.

Before going any further, I should like to say: please read the maker's instructions very carefully and carry them out in every respect.

The effect of acid eating into the glass is to produce a pearly, matt surface. The theory is that all parts of the glass which are not to be touched by the acid must be masked in some way. Industrially, the masking can be done with a coating of special wax, which is then cut away in areas which are to be patterned by the acid.

There are various ways of achieving the same results at home. The masking is done by using the kind of adhesive plastic which is sold in rolls for use on kitchen shelves, tabletops, etc. It is known by different names in different places (for example, Fablon or Contact in Britain, contact paper in the USA). The design is cut out of the paper.

In addition to this adhesive plastic covering, which should be in a plain colour, you will need a small sharp tool for cutting. This can be a craft knife, a scalpel or any other suitable cutting edge.

First, trace or draw your chosen design on to a piece of tracing paper, then cut a piece of contact paper larger than the design. If the piece of glass is shaped, allow for this when cutting the contact paper so that when it is applied to the glass it does not 'pleat' at the edges.

Next, shade with wax pencil on the reverse side of the tracing and retrace the design on to the contact paper. You can use small pieces of masking tape to hold the tracing paper firmly to the contact paper while you are doing the retracing.

Having now got a traced design on the contact paper, gently peel away the paper backing and fix the contact paper to the glass. Make sure that it has been applied smoothly and that there are no wrinkles.

With the knife or chosen cutting tool now cut very carefully round the edges of the design, taking care not to get any ragged edges and not to cut beyond lines or angles. When the cutting has been completed, take the tip of the blade and very gently ease up the edges of each piece which has to be removed; peel off these cut-away pieces. You will be left with a cut out stencil on the glass, to which the etching paste is applied. Before applying the paste, examine all the edges of the design to make sure that they are adhering tightly to the surface of the glass. Press the contact paper down very firmly, but in doing so be careful not to stretch the cut edges.

Now follow the instructions for using the etching paste. The recommended minimum time of three minutes will give a soft matt surface. If you wish to etch more than one glass with the same design, peel the contact paper very carefully from the glass so that it can be used again. This can be done several times.

If you have only used one application of the etching cream and have a lightly matted surface, you can then use this as a base for engraving. For example, you can outline the etching by engraving a narrow border round the design with a drill and a fine diamond burr. This can also be done with a diamond hand tool if you have no drill – just scratch a narrow border round the design. As well as applying engraved outlines (these show up much whiter than the etching) you can also engrave patterns within the etched areas.

Etching can be used in many ways in conjunction with both diamond point work and that done with a drill. A lightly etched area can be stippled afterwards, or it can be used as a base for further drill engraving. There are many possibilities and it is well worthwhile experimenting first on a cheap glass.

You can also use etching cream if you have a fairly large area of some design which has to be matted. In this case, masking is probably not practicable and you must trust to your own skill simply to paint the cream on with a fine brush over the areas in question. If you use this method, watch the work carefully during the three minutes wait because when there is no masking the cream sometimes has a tendency to trickle beyond the area you have painted. If this looks like happening you can steer the cream back on course with a brush.

When the waiting time is up, wash the cream off very quickly.

Etching cream can also create cloud effects. It should simply be painted on where necessary, with no masking. The results are necessarily somewhat unpredictable, so practise first on an old glass.

An etched surface responds extremely well and very quickly to polishing. All methods are effective. So, with an etched area as a starting base, many different effects can be built up by the use of both engraving and polishing.

Another glass etching process, newly developed in Britain, is a Glass Etching Kit, which is described as safe to use – the fluid, the makers say, is harmless. For suppliers see Appendix. This is a different process because the mask is not applied in the form of cut out designs which you make yourself. Instead, a special thick masking fluid is supplied with the kit. This is painted on to the glass first. Then, when it is completely dry, the design is drawn on to it and gently scraped away so that glass is exposed. The etching fluid is then applied to the exposed areas of glass and left on for a recommended period.

Gilding

Over the centuries, gilding has sometimes been sparingly used in conjunction with engraving. Nowadays there is an excellent liquid gilt available, which is sold under the name of Treasure Gold Liquid Leaf. A clear sealer, which helps to extend the life of the gilt, is also available. When you use gilding and in what amount, is really a matter of taste. It would, I think, be asking too much of any unfired process to use it on anything which needs constant washing, although Liquid Leaf with sealer applied is waterproof.

If you are interested in trying out the effect of a little gilding, just bear in mind that it is a waste of time to apply it over painstaking stippling. Some interesting results can be obtained, though, if it is applied over line work or drill engraving. It sinks into the tiny grooves made by the lines and gives a rather delicate effect. If using it in this way, apply the Liquid Leaf quickly and, with an absorbent but lint-free cloth, at once wipe over the surface you have painted. This will remove all the paint except that which has sunk into the lines. The same process should be used when applying the sealer.

Another use of gilding is as part of a general pattern, applied separately as part of the pattern and not actually over an engraved area.

The solvent for Liquid Leaf is methylated spirit (denatured alcohol) so use this to clean brushes and then wash them in warm, soapy water.

Colouring

There are various transparent glass paints available which do not need firing and these can be bought from art or craft shops. One excellent make is Deka. Although this does not necessarily require firing, it can, in fact, be baked at a very low temperature in an ordinary domestic oven. This makes it more permanent.

There is a growing interest in the use of colour with glasswork of all kinds and you might wish to experiment with some. The amount you use and the occasions when you use it are really a matter of personal choice. One very effective way of doing so is as part of a general and rather intricate design, as seen in the photograph of work by Majella Taylor (plate 31). Although this is not reproduced in colour, it is still possible to get a general idea of the way in which it was used.

If you want to use colour yourself, primary colours which can be mixed will probably be more use than a larger range of ready-mixed shades so, unless you already know exactly which ones you want, it might be as well to get, say, yellow, red, light blue and dark blue. You also need thinner for mixing the colours. Good instructions are included with the paints.

If the colours are applied without dilution, they are quite rich and dark, rather like stained glass windows. The addition of a little thinner makes them more transparent. As baking is intended to increase their durability, it is as well to do this, and provided the glass is put into a cold oven at first the risk to it should not be great. It is shock, not heat, that makes glass crack. However, if you have any doubt about the temperature of your oven, it would be safer to test it with an oven thermometer. Allow the glass to cool completely before handling it and taking it out of the oven. The solvent for Deka is either the thinner or acetone (nail polish remover). Either of these can be used for cleaning brushes. After cleaning, wash the brushes in warm, soapy water.

These colours can not only be applied after engraving has been done but may be applied first and engraved over afterwards.

Sandblasting

This is an almost instant method of matting the surface of glass by means of blasting fine grit on to it under pressure. The glass must be masked where no matting is required. If the sandblasting process is applied long enough and with sufficient pressure the glass can be so worn away that the masked areas can be left standing away from the rest of the glass. These areas can then be engraved, with very interesting results.

The best equipment for home use is that obtainable from a dental-tool supplier, but it is expensive. A smaller, cheaper tool which can be used for light work is an abrasive spray; it works on the principle of an airbrush and is obtainable from good craft stores.

Postscript

If, as I hope, you find engraving enjoyable, there are a few more points that you need to know.

The first is: sign and date your work. It is not only often useful to know when you engraved a particular piece of glass, but it is also essential if the work has been commissioned or is to be exhibited. Glassware should be signed under the base, and anything else in a suitably inconspicuous place.

The next is: always confirm commissions *in writing* – even if you know the person well. Do not only confirm the date by which an engraving is required; if necessary, confirm when it is *not* required. For example, if someone says emphatically 'Of course I don't want this before Christmas', be sure to put that in writing. If possible, where initials and/or dates are ordered, get the other person to write out exactly what is required.

Another point: as you begin to receive commissions you will probably be worried about what to charge. This is a very difficult matter in the early days. But do not charge too little. It is unfair to those whose livelihood depends upon engraving to undersell just because, for you, it may simply be a little extra cash. If your work is worth buying, it is worth the appropriate price and the buyer will think less of it if it was sold cheaply. That's human nature!

Finally, always deliver work on time and packed as attractively as possible.

3
Photographing Engraved Glass

It can be very satisfying to possess good photographs of examples of your work which you have enjoyed doing. You may feel something has turned out particularly well; perhaps the design or the method of engraving you have used has been especially successful. Then it all goes beyond your reach because the glass was a present or a commission and someone else now possesses it. All you are left with is a fading memory of what it looked like. So photographs of your own work are not only a pleasure as recollections but can also be a very useful record for future reference. If, for example, you had worked on a complete set of glasses, you might be asked to engrave a replacement for a broken one. A photographic record would then be not only invaluable but probably essential. But even if you did not wish to reproduce a former design exactly, it is often helpful to look through records of past work in order to see if old designs can be developed into something new. Photographs can often remind you, too, of the sources of designs – sources from which more ideas may flow for new projects. If your work increases in quantity you may need some kind of brochure, and in this case good photographs are a necessity.

This chapter is intended for amateur photographers and has been written with invaluable advice and guidance from Ian Gorf. I hope it will help many people to venture upon trying their hand at photographing their work because the high cost of having this done professionally often rules it out. There are obviously several other ways of photographing engraved glass successfully and you will no doubt work out yours by trial and error. The methods described for taking photographs of studio standard are those always used by Ian Gorf, some of whose work illustrates this book.

In writing this chapter I have had two typical situations in mind. The first is those who cannot afford an expensive camera and who realise that close-up photographs of studio quality cannot be achieved. Nevertheless, some kind of record of their work would be useful. So into this category fall what I call simple 'snapshots': nothing elaborate but just a record of your work for your personal use and clear enough to remind you how the engraving was done. The second category of photograph is for those who want a better-quality result, a close-up in fact, producing something which would be suitable for a portfolio of work or which could be reproduced in a brochure.

Taking the photographs is, of course, only part of the story. While I believe that many people either possess, or would be prepared to buy, a suitable camera for one or other category of photograph, I feel that most would be reluctant to go further along the road of home photography and invest in all the equipment necessary to develop and print their own work. This really involves learning a whole new skill. Apart, too, from taking up a great deal of time, it also involves creating some kind of darkroom, however temporary, and in many cases this is simply not possible in one's home surroundings. So the methods of taking photographs and the types of camera suggested in the following paragraphs are all described on the assumption that you will have your photographs developed commercially, which is usually quite satisfactory.

Simple 'Snapshots'

CAMERAS

The kind of camera which can cope with simple photographs comes into what, even at today's prices, is considered as the moderate-to-cheap range. That being so, there are probably many people who already have such a camera but have not attempted to tackle glass as a subject because they do not know how to set it up or illuminate it, to display its special characteristics. Others may feel that they would have additional uses for a moderately priced camera and would be prepared to buy one.

Cameras in this category can be any type of fixed lens camera, and this includes Polaroid. The only essential requirement is that it should have a focussing mechanism which is adjustable for distance

PLATES

Plate 21　*Old Age Looking Back*, a drill engraving by Ann Dybka consisting of three panels, one behind another *(Gervais Purcell)*
1st panel – old man, and tree with climbing 'old man's beard'
2nd panel – youth in his prime, with roses at base
3rd panel – childhood
Plate 22　Cullet by Barbara Norman, drill engraved on front, back and one side
Plate 23　*The London Scene* sketch done by Pat Robinson with Burgess Engraver
Plate 24　Two decanters, drill engraved by Barbara Norman
Plate 25　Engraved by Majella Taylor with a Burgess Engraver
Plate 26　Engraved by Peter Pullan with a Burgess Engraver
Plate 27　Flat dish engraved by Peter Pullan with a Burgess Engraver
Plate 28　An example of decorative initialling, by Stephen Rickard *(A.C. Cooper Ltd)*
Plate 29　Wineglass with diamond engraved inscription and calligraphic scroll work. Dutch, c1660 *Crown Copyright. Victoria and Albert Museum*
Plate 30　Drill engraving by Denis Bustard using 'Letraset' for lettering
Plate 31　Panel by Majella Taylor using colour with engraving
Plate 32　Window in St John's Church, St John's, near Woking, Surrey; drill engraved and polished by Anne Cotton
Plate 33　Decorative lettering. Drill engraving by Eric Smith
Plate 34　Presentation box – made by Denis Bustard
Plate 35　*Pastoral* jug. Male and female mythical creatures and a pair of cornucopiae flanking a vernal mask. Diamond wheel engraved and polished by Stephen Rickard *(A.C. Cooper Ltd)*
Plate 36　*The Music of Chalk.* Stipple engraving by Laurence Whistler
Plate 37　Engraved by Elly Eliades using diamond point, diamond-impregnated wheels, carborundum wheels and burrs, Burgess drill with tungsten tips; and finally polished
Plate 38　Tim Appleyard at work on the Arundel Cathedral Goblet
Plate 39　Arundel Cathedral. Drill engraved goblet by Tim Appleyard, which was presented to the President of Kenya
Plate 40　Windows in the chapel of the Convent of Poor Clares, Arundel, Sussex. Drill engraved by Sister Giles
Plate 41　Engraved with Burgess Professional Engraver by Peter Pullan

22

23

24

Majella 1972

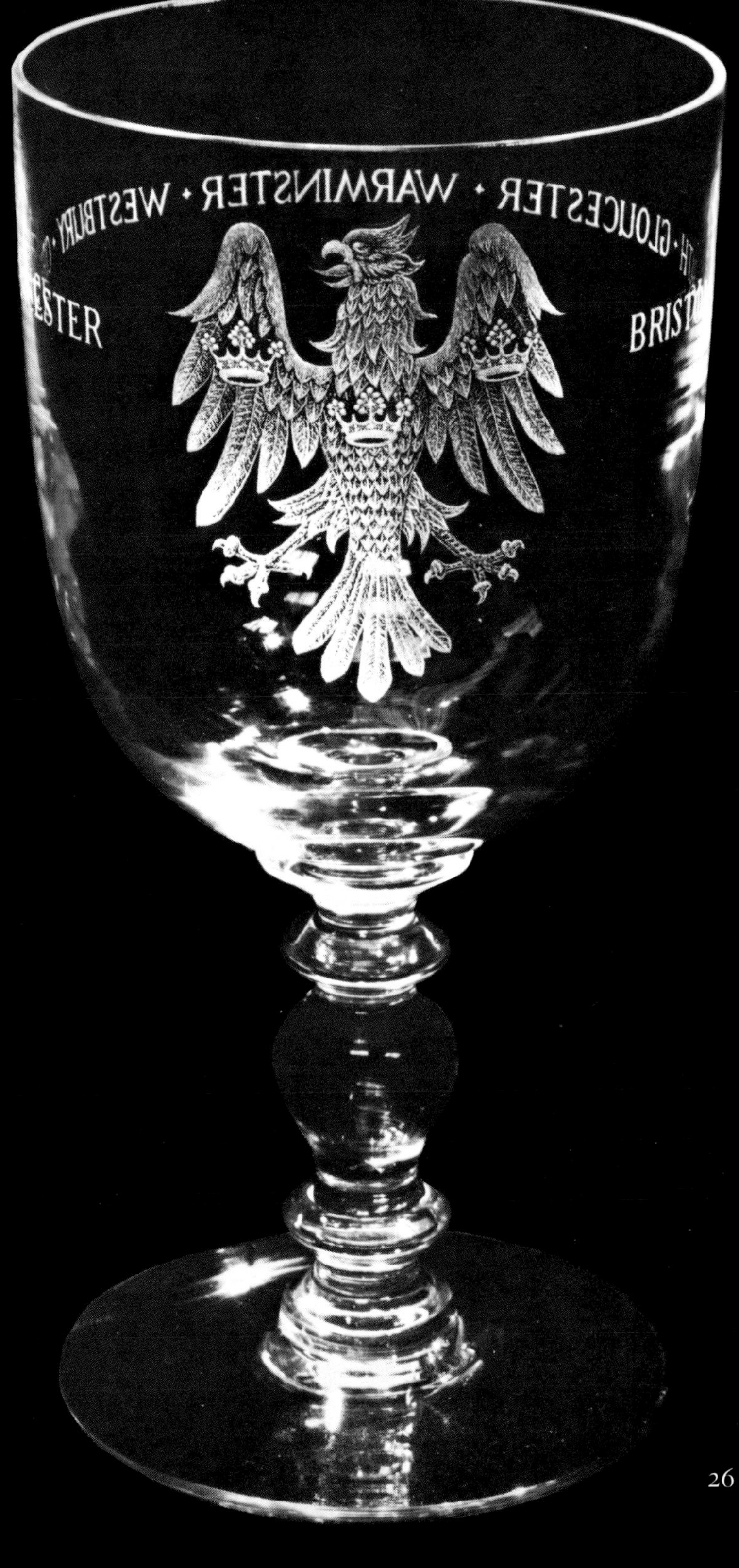

26

27

28

34

35

38

39

40

and which can be set for a minimum distance of approximately 1m (3ft) so that the engraving can be recorded as sharply as possible. If the camera does not have distances marked on the focussing ring, it may be equipped with symbols which give some indication of distance to enable the sharpest possible picture to be taken.

EXPOSURE

Exposure of the film is important and cannot be judged accurately by guesswork so some kind of light metering is necessary. Many cameras, even in the moderate price range, already have built-in metering. This may be manual, automatic or both, which is an advantage. In all cases, of course, they also have exposure values (apertures and speeds) shown on the camera and these can be adjusted according to the indication given by the metering system. If the camera you are using does not have an integral meter and has to be adjusted manually, a separate hand-held meter should be used. A slight problem can arise with a hand-held meter if you are using artificial lighting to illuminate the work, since the meter could give a reading based on the brightness of the lights rather than on the brightness of the object to be photographed. To eliminate this, hold the meter as close to the glass as possible without causing a shadow to fall upon the glass.

If the camera is fully automatic, you need do nothing about exposure or metering as this is all done for you mechanically or electronically.

Where the camera can be used either manually or automatically, you need to make an exposure reading by taking the camera to within a distance of about 30cm (1ft) or slightly less from the object and adjust for the correct exposure regardless of the lights being used. Then go back away from the object to a distance of about 1m (3ft) and the exposure you have set will still be correct.

To make sure of the exposure, you might think it worthwhile taking three photographs – one at the exposure you have set and the other two at one aperture more and one aperture less.

SHUTTER SPEED

Cameras in the cheap-to-moderate range with fixed focal length lenses (ie which cannot be adjusted for either distance or aperture) usually have only one shutter speed. You will not get very satisfactory results with these – only a very limited reminder to yourself of the general appearance of the work. Of course, the results obtained from such simple cameras can be greatly assisted by good setting up and lighting of the glass.

If your camera can be adjusted for speed and if a tripod is unobtainable, start by trying a speed of 1/60th of a second in good light – either full daylight or good artificial lighting. This is the slowest speed at which it is advisable to hold the camera by hand to get a sharp picture, and then only if you have steady hands. If you decide to use a slower speed than this you should use a tripod and a shutter release. A sharper picture could be obtained by setting the aperture to f.8 and giving a longer exposure, say one second.

Studio-quality Photographs

Photographs of this standard obviously require a camera and lens which are more expensive and which can be adjusted to deal with distance, speed and aperture. It is an advantage if the camera is also equipped with an interchangeable lens. The importance of this is the opportunity for greater focal length which means you can still get a close-up of the object even if you are further away from it. Such a lens does not distort the object as much as taking the photograph with the camera closer to the object and using a lens with a shorter focal length.

If a close-up of a very small object is desired, an extension tube can be used. It would then be possible to photograph at a distance of only 8–10cm (3–4in) from the object.

It is very useful to establish early on what the best conditions are for your photography of glass – the best setting, lighting and general lay-out – so that you can go on using the same equipment and arrangement. This may, initially, mean several trial runs until you finally achieve satisfactory results, but in the end it will save a great deal of effort.

FILM

The kind of photographs which you can take is determined by the films most readily available: ie prints in black and white by both daylight and artificial light, and prints in colour by daylight only. Transparencies in colour can be taken in daylight or artificial light.

For taking *black and white prints* with most types of camera, any of the major makes of 35mm film is suitable. These are sold in 12, 20 and 36 exposures. There is no advantage in any particular number of exposures so long as you can keep an accurate record of the conditions under which you took each photograph. It is no help to look at some prints afterwards and see that one was wrong but have no record of what you used. For taking black and white prints indoors in good daylight, a film with ASA between 125 and 200 is suitable. If the level of light is low, try a faster film with ASA 400. For *colour prints* taken in similar daylight conditions, the same ASA values apply.

If you want a *black and white transparency*, follow the directions for taking a black and white print and ask for it to be made into a transparency when you take the film for processing. If you are taking *colour transparencies* any good make of film is suitable. In daylight use a film with a speed of ASA 200 or 400. If you are taking colour transparencies in artificial light you must use a tungsten-light film. This is because it is balanced for special photographic bulbs (see page 101).

Setting Up

It might almost be said that the setting up of the glass to be photographed and the illumination you choose is more important than the camera. However splendid the camera, you cannot hope to get a good photograph if the light is either inadequate or if it comes from the wrong direction and results in the engraved glass being obscured by a mass of reflections. For this reason, if you can possibly manage to use a good daylight rather than artificial light you will usually achieve better results. Daylight, if it is used correctly, gives a uniform, soft illumination and there are few, if any, reflections. And daylight does not mean direct sunlight. If you try to use sunlight as the source of illumination you can be confronted with very bright reflections on the glass, and somehow all reflections always seem to be multiplied into unbelievable brilliance in the final print.

USING DAYLIGHT

Again, the simplest and – if it is used properly – best kind of light in which to photograph glass is good daylight. It is best to have the source of light above and behind the glass, although you may want to experiment with letting some additional light come from the sides.

This way of using daylight for illumination need not be very complicated in ordinary domestic surroundings, which are the ones I have in mind. To achieve a source of daylight from behind the glass to be photographed the obvious need is a good-sized window.

Engraved glass shows up best if arranged against a background which is both dark and matt. Black is excellent – probably best. But if you are taking colour prints or transparencies and want a coloured background, try a very dark colour. (This can be whatever you wish, of course, but bear in mind that some colours can change tone and appear to be lighter in artificial light.)

So, first you will need something to form a dark, matt background. This could be a piece of cloth – without any sheen at all – or paper. You will also need something dark and matt (preferably the same material as the background) upon which to stand the glass.

To deal with the background: fix the cloth or paper across the

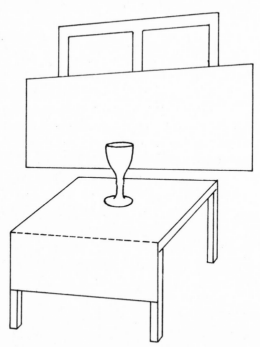

Using daylight and masking a window with black cloth or paper. Glass is displayed on flat surface covered with black cloth or paper

100

lower half of the window. It should be of sufficient depth to form a background of the required height for the piece of glass, but must at the same time leave as large an area as possible of the window unmasked so that the maximum amount of light will shine down upon the piece of engraved glass. If the window has side angles, you may wish to mask these too, in order to cut out side lighting. In front of the window place a table or anything else which is suitable for the glass to stand upon. This should be near enough to the window to receive the maximum amount of daylight. Cover the table with matt dark cloth or paper and stand the glass upon it. Move the glass around until the maximum amount of light falls upon it, and display it well against a dark background. If you have a long enough piece of cloth or paper for the background this can simply be extended down from the window and over the table in one continuous sweep. If you want no side lighting the cloth should be as wide as the window. Make sure that, viewed from camera level, there is no break between background and base – just one continuous area of dark material. The best level for the camera is the same level as the glass.

USING ARTIFICIAL LIGHT

If you want to use artificial lighting as the source of illumination, you should always use photographic bulbs and not ordinary domestic ones. This is in order to avoid a colourcast, the result of which turns the entire photograph orange/red. The worst kind of illumination is electric lighting directed straight on to the engraved glass. This will cause a great deal of reflection.

There are some simple ways of overcoming this. In each case, dark surroundings are necessary, so take the photographs after dark without any daylight in the room at all.

The first method involves the use of a piece of flat glass and two bases of equal height (such as two small tables, two upturned boxes – even two upright chairs). You also need an electric lamp with an approximately 275–500 watt bulb. This can be either an adjustable-angle desk lamp or an ordinary short reading lamp. If you are using the latter, you must remove the shade.

First, place the two bases far enough apart to be able to stand your chosen lamp between them. If you are using a reading lamp, the bases should be a little taller than the lamp because the aim is to shine light upwards between them. If you have to use bases which are

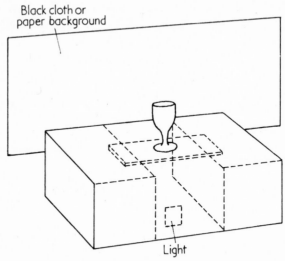

Using artificial light. Glass sheet rests on two bases of equal height and all is covered with black cloth or paper, down to floor level. Hole is cut for light, goblet is placed over hole. Light source is below, as indicated

Using artificial light (alternative method). Box is covered with black cloth or paper to floor level. Goblet stands over hole, light source is below as indicated

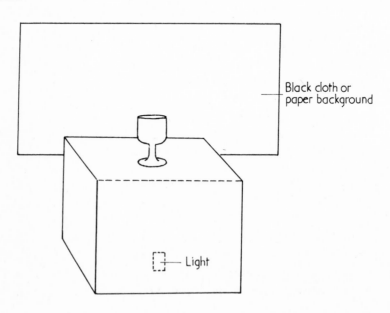

much higher than the lamp, you will also have to place the lamp on something so that its light is not too far away from the top level of the base. An angled lamp must be twisted so that its light is directed upwards.

Having positioned the source of light correctly between the two bases, place the piece of flat glass across the gap between them. Cover bases and glass with dark paper; place more paper to conceal the lamp. Cut a small hole in the paper in the place where the glass will stand. The light will shine upwards through this and illuminate the glass from below. Before taking photographs you may have to adjust the strength of the light. A final point is to check that there is nothing in the background which shows up even dimly in the small amount of light you are using.

Another method of using artificial light is really a variation on what has already been described but it uses different 'props'.

If you cannot provide two bases of equal height upon which to stand a piece of flat glass, you can make do with something else such as a large but sturdy cardboard box. As well as being strong, this must also be large enough to contain the lighting you use and to provide enough space and air round the light in order to avoid over-heating. The idea is the same: to shine light upwards on to the glass.

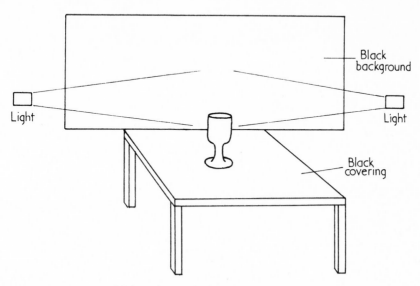

Using electric lighting behind glass

103

The difference is that in this case it shines up through a hole cut in the box. This method is somewhat primitive and much depends upon the box being both strong and level.

A third method uses electric lights in a different way: side and back lighting which is directed *behind* the glass. For this method you need, as before, a matt dark background and base. The glass should stand sufficiently far in front of the background to enable a light placed at either side to shine behind the glass. In order to make full use of the light and to concentrate it on the object to be photographed, it is helpful to make funnel-shaped shades from aluminium foil. These need not necessarily be narrow. Experiment until you have achieved the best shape and size. Foil shades are also useful because they help to increase the light by means of reflection.

4
Displaying Engraved Glass

Engraved glass gains almost more by good display than a picture does by being framed. In fact, much stipple engraving is almost invisible unless it is displayed under suitable conditions. There may be occasions when you will wish to show your work to its greatest advantage, and some idea of the ways in which this can be done may be useful. It is surprising how few galleries – or even major museums – have any experience of what is required or, worse still, have no ideas about what to do when confronted with glass to be displayed.

You may want to show your glass advantageously in your own home. If you feel you have done some good or interesting work, it is a pleasure as well as an encouragement to see it well displayed in your home surroundings. If people want you to do engravings for them and you begin to get commissions, then a few well-displayed pieces are essential. Sometimes you may find that someone wants to buy one of your display pieces, but they are more usually the basis of ideas on the part of the customer – for example, a particular design may be very much liked but you may be asked to engrave it on different glass. Either way, it is very important to have examples of your work available and expertly displayed. Incidentally, for the benefit of potential customers, it is always a good idea to have some unengraved glass attractively set out, as well as your own examples of engraving. People are often first attracted by a particular piece of glass and then enjoy planning a design as the next stage in commissioning an engraving.

If you are beginning to reach a good standard of work, you may find that one of your local shops, or perhaps a small gallery, will be willing to display some of your engravings for sale. This kind of situation can often present the greatest problems and be the most disheartening of all. It really does require firmness, but backed up by some knowledge, to deal with it both tactfully and successfully. After all, not only you but the shop or gallery, too, wish the work to find buyers.

Sometimes you may find that you are able to team up with other engravers and so be able to stage a somewhat larger exhibition of your combined work. This presents yet another situation, which can be dealt with in other ways.

Display in Your Home or Studio

The simplest way of all to display engraved glass is against daylight, although of course this does mean that it is only seen to its full advantage during the day. If you are unable to set up any special artificial lighting for your glass, this may prove to be a useful way of overcoming the problem to some extent. In the case of panels, and indeed of windows, this is the way in which they were intended to be viewed.

However, if you are not using daylight as the source of illumination, there are various other methods of display. One is to use a dark, or at least dim, area and then to illuminate the glass. It is unlikely that you can provide *very* dim surroundings either in your home or studio, but at least you can try to position the glass so that the lighting you provide for it is not in competition with other general lighting in the room. Choose a part of the room which normally has the least amount of light. The glass will need basically two things: a black background and either upward or downward lighting directed upon it. If possible, use a fluorescent tube for this and not a filament bulb. (Fluorescent lighting is, in any case, cooler and if the light is positioned near the glass, this is an advantage.) If you are displaying only one piece of glass, this can be done very successfully by making a suitable-sized box and lining it with matt black material – either velvet or flock paper. Then light the glass either from above or below. Before deciding whether upward or downward lighting is best, experiment with both. If you decide that you are going to use upward lighting, you will also have to experiment with both a slit and a hole for the light to shine through, and determine beforehand the size of whichever you choose.

Ideally, the display box should be completely enclosed, with a glass front, as this will help to keep the engraved glass inside it free from dust. However, if all this really does prove to be beyond your resources you will have to try to provide just the minimum – a single source of light and a dark background.

Display in Galleries or Shops

If you are offered the opportunity to show some of your work in a gallery or shop, it is essential to find out how and where it will be displayed. Do not leave everything to them. In your early days as an engraver you may well feel that they are the experts and must surely know best. You may be reticent about making your views known, and in any case, with little experience, you may not yet have many views. But it is a great disappointment, and, indeed, unnerving, to go along on private view day and find that all your hard work is almost invisible. If your work is bold in appearance, done with a drill, for example, the problem of display may perhaps not be quite so serious, but if you have done any stipple engraving this will need very careful presentation. Very few shops or galleries have had any experience of exhibiting engraved glass and most are glad to discuss the matter with you. Often, what at first seems a very unpromising situation can be turned into success once it is clear exactly what is needed. But it is sensible to bear in mind that it will be no help to you if your work is not seen to advantage – or, as in the case of really bad display, is not seen at all.

First of all, it really is essential to make sure that the area itself is as dim as possible. No matter how much black background and black base you can arrange, or how many individual lights are at your disposal, you will achieve very little if you are in competition with bright, general, overhead lighting. This really is the heart of the problem – a dim area – because naturally the gallery/shop will want all its other displays in well illuminated surroundings. However, as no one else will be aiming for a dim area, you might even find that your need of this can be turned into an advantage. You might be able to use such unlikely places as a staircase, an entrance hall, or some dark unused corner, and so turn such an area into a positive – and unexpected – attraction; an advantage not only to yourself but to the gallery/shop also.

Try to discuss the whole question of display well ahead and if you are not given a suitably dim area, decide how best you can create one by, for example, using sheets of black paper to screen off some unwanted light. You will almost certainly find you need extra individual lights in specific positions and this may involve some minor electrical work being done. It is immensely worrying to find that you need extra plugs or lead with, perhaps, no means of obtaining either. So work out first exactly what you will require in the way of black paper, black cloth, masking tape, electrical fittings, and so on. If you want to display your work in the best possible conditions, proper display cabinets are the answer. These can, of course, be any size and should, as already described, be equipped with either upward or downward lighting. If you begin to exhibit work frequently, you may think it worthwhile building (or having built) your own transportable display cabinet. In this case, as it will have to cope with pieces of glass of different shapes and sizes, and perhaps also with work of varying techniques, fluorescent strip lighting placed above is likely to be more generally effective than a source of light from below.

If you are showing work in a shop you may simply be allocated some shelf space. With luck, the shelves themselves may be made of glass. In this case, make a dark background with black paper, put more black paper on one shelf and cut a hole or slit in this for the light to shine through and then place a light on the lower shelf so that it shines through the hole/slit and up through your glass. Do not forget, though, that the light itself must be screened off from view. If your glass needs a downward light you can use the same principle, simply reversing the process and shining the light down on to it through a glass shelf above.

If none of the above suggestions can be carried out, there is one last possibility: try to arrange back lighting. To do this, provide a black background and black base for the glass. Then arrange a source of light either from one side or both sides so that it shines behind the glass. It may be necessary to experiment with foil shades in order to direct the light as required. Consider, also, the possibility of getting a piece of clear plastic (less heavy than glass) cut to size, and taping it to both shelves so that it makes a box for your work. This will protect it from dust.

Finally, make sure that your work has been displayed the right way up and the right way round. This may sound obvious, but, believe me, it needs watching! If you have engraved a glass block, for example, which is meant to be displayed standing up, it is quite a shock to find that it has been placed flat down (probably on a light surface), thus making the engraving barely visible. As for displaying work the right way round, this applies, of course, to any round piece of glass with the engraving done in reverse on the far side, which you are intended to look at *through* the glass. Just check that the glass has been correctly positioned: it is easy for someone else to make a mistake.

Mounting an Exhibition

If you are combining with other engravers and have sufficient work to form a complete exhibition, the situation may be somewhat easier because you are then in a position to occupy a separate room or area. The same considerations of lighting apply as have already been suggested, but with a whole room at your disposal the major problem of dim general lighting is much easier to solve.

5
Packing Engraved Glass

Packing your engraved glass can be thought of in two ways: either packaging it attractively in boxes suitable for presentation, or literally packing it for postage. The following are some suggestions for both methods. They are used successfully by many people but, of course, there can be no *guarantee* that glass will not break in the post. However, glass has to be conveyed somehow and, barring unforeseen hazards, these methods are worth trying.

To deal first with packing for postage, it is essential always to send glass by letter post and not by parcel post if size permits. If you send a package by parcel post, you will have to make it absolutely crush-proof because anything, of any vast weight or size, may crash down upon it. Just imagine a piece of heavy machinery, for instance, landing on your comparatively small parcel of engraved glass and you will realise the degree of protection which would be necessary. Of course, even if you are sending it by letter post it must be extremely carefully packed and protected as quite a heavy weight may still fall upon it.

The first method is one which is often used by glass manufacturers themselves. You need a box which is considerably larger than the glass it is to contain. A cardboard box is quite adequate provided it is extremely strong. I do not mean the kind which you might get from a supermarket and which has contained groceries but, rather, one which you might get from an off-licence or liquor store and which was designed to contain heavy bottles. These latter are usually very strong. If you can acquire (perhaps from a local store) a polystyrene box, that would be best of all. These boxes are not only intended especially for glass or china but are extremely light in weight. Packing material can consist of quite a variety of materials, either used separately or mixed as you wish. Manufacturers of glass often use any of the following: wood-wool, polystyrene granules, plastic sheets with air bubbles, or shredded paper. Used carefully, all are excellent.

Obtaining these materials is something which needs some organising. It is not usually possible to buy them because they are sold in bulk and few engravers need such large quantities. So, first of all, save any packing materials which come your way. Save all tissue paper – even if this is crumpled the creases can be ironed out very easily. And, of course, save any suitable boxes. If you buy glass from a local source, explain why you need it and ask the store if they can spare you any packing material from time to time. Most are helpful, and, in any case, they usually receive far more than they use. If every source of supply fails, you can, with a certain amount of effort, make your own shredded paper. This is easily done, of course, if you have access to a shredder. However, few people are so fortunate and it is quite possible to make your own either by cutting newspaper into strips about 18mm (¾in) wide or by tearing it up into small pieces. You will need a lot.

Before you pack any engraved glass in the box you have chosen, the glass itself must be well wrapped in at least two thicknesses of tissue paper. Lead crystal, in particular, is easily scratched and some of the packing materials could well do this if the glass is not properly protected. All shapes (except decanters) must themselves be tightly filled with packing material. Line them first with tissue paper to prevent scratching (coloured paper will show up the engraving) and then press packing material very firmly into them. If you are packing glass in this way simply for postage, you are not giving it any presentation. However, you can certainly improve the appearance of the general packing if you wrap the glass in coloured tissue paper. Choose a strong or dark colour; this helps to dramatise the engraving. For extra protection against scratching, put a few more layers of tissue paper below and above the glass. Lastly, fill the box *very tightly* with the packing material. Press it well down all round the sides and into the corners, and end with a thick layer on top. By this time the contents of the box should be totally immovable and the lid should press down firmly upon the filling.

If you are packing a decanter for postage, remember that the most vulnerable part is the neck. So take particular care to place the decan-

111

ter in such a position that an extra amount of packing material can be tightly rammed down between the neck and the side of the box. The stopper must be wrapped separately, first in tissue paper and then in a good layer of packing material or corrugated cardboard. When packing it in the box, care should be taken to separate it from the decanter with a good layer of packing material. It is wise to put a note in a conspicuous position inside the box saying that the contents are a decanter *and* stopper.

One method of packing glass for presentation and not for postage is to keep the glass firmly positioned away from the sides of the box. It is not easy to achieve if you have to find your own high-quality cardboard boxes and cut the right-sized interiors, and some people may find it easier to buy these ready to assemble (for supplier see page 181). However, if you want to make a simple cardboard presentation box, the following method can be used. You will need a box which looks good enough for the purpose. If it does not, cover it with suitable paper. Next, take a firm piece of cardboard. Rule on to it a shape which is the *exact* size of the base of the box. Then extend these ruled lines as shown in the diagram, making them the same length as the height at which the glass is to be positioned above the base of the box. Cut out the shape. With a sharp knife or single-edged razor blade, score the lines forming the measurements of the box (dotted lines in the diagram). When the extensions are bent back along the scored lines you will have a false base for the box. This should fit it exactly. Before bending back the extensions, you must cut out a shape which fits the glass so that it can be held in position.

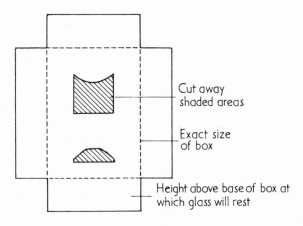

112

To do this, draw round the glass as shown in the diagram, making a small lip at the top which will fit down into the bowl. Cut out this shape with a craft knife. Line the base of the box with dark flock paper. Cover the top of the false base with this too, cutting away the shape for the glass. Put the false base in the box and fit the glass carefully into the cut out shape. The glass will be firmly held in position and will show up well against the dark flock background.

MAKING SPECIAL BOXES

Another very effective and rather more lavish way of packing both for presentation and for postage is in specially made, lined wooden boxes. As well as being sturdy enough to be sent through the post, they display engraved glass to great advantage and turn what might be a slightly amateurish effort into something thoroughly professional. I am assured that if you have any skill with carpentry they are not at all difficult to make. As I am no carpenter myself, I can do no better than let Denis Bustard (who is!) explain the method he uses with such success. So, in his words:

The appearance of a piece of engraved glass can be greatly improved by bedding it in silk or velvet in its own box. This not only presents a good general effect, but by adjusting the angle of the piece in its 'nest', the engraving itself can be emphasised. Showing the glass in this way does, moreover, discourage casual handling.

Such boxes can often be made by modifying existing containers but for really important occasions one may wish to make a special box, particularly if the object is heavy and needs to be held securely.

Presentation boxes of the highest standard can in fact be made with quite simple materials such as plywood, vinyl, black velvet, and small brass hinges and clasps.

9mm five-ply is used for the base of such a box and 7mm three-ply for the sides and top. Glue and panel pins are sufficient to hold it all together. It is best not to make the top and bottom halves separately, but rather first to build the whole box completely, including closing in the top. When the glue has hardened, cut the box in half laterally. Top and bottom halves will thus match up perfectly when they come together again.

The vinyl should be cut into long strips and glued right round the front, sides and back of each half of the box with a generous overlap to fold into the interior and over on to the top or bottom of the box. The vinyl is easy to cut so take care of corners and edges; it will stretch a little where necessary and even compress slightly.

The top surface of the upper half of the box so far formed has vinyl coming up over the edges with bare wood showing over most of the area. This can be covered with a piece of vinyl cut so that it comes within about 1mm of the edge. A more professional touch can be achieved, however, if a thick card just longer and wider than the box is covered with vinyl and then glued to the top of the box.

The underside of the lower half of the box can be covered with vinyl, felt or baize to within about 2mm of the edge.

Very small brass hinges, clasps and pins are supplied in packets at good hardware shops and when fitted they lend a real air to the box and play an important role in the general appearance of the whole.

The following sketch and notes may help to explain some of the things which have been described so far.

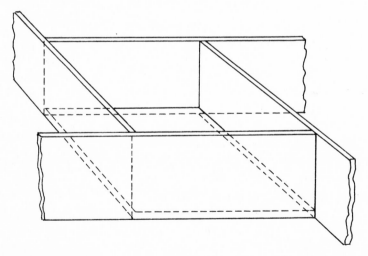

Box Construction
The base and sides should be pinned and glued as shown. When the glue has hardened, the ends which protrude can be sawn off.

It may not be great cabinet-making but it produces a good result and makes for reasonable accuracy.

The top is then cut to a size about 5mm wider and longer than the box and glued and pinned into position so that there is a slight overlap all round. When the glue has dried, the overlap can be planed down until one has a perfectly plain, closed-in box ready for the next stage of cutting into its upper and lower parts.

Hinges

The sketch shows how the hinges can be fixed in position quickly and easily. A cabinet-maker would tuck the flaps of the hinges between the top and bottom halves of the box but for our purposes the hinges can be attached externally as shown. The spine of each hinge will nestle snugly into the space between the two halves of the box and this will help to line up the hinge while the pins are being hammered in.

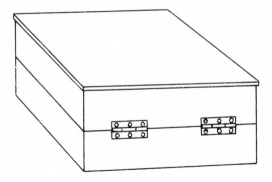

Vinyl Covering

The vinyl referred to is the type which forms the smooth 'skin' on many modern wallpapers. It is necessary to strip the vinyl skin from the paper since the wallpaper itself is too stiff for our purposes. The best way of doing this is first to cut the wallpaper into the size of strips you will need to cover the box, and then to paste these strips on a board. After an hour or so, scratch away at a corner of the vinyl to separate it from its paper backing and then carefully peel it off.

Whichever method of packing you use, there is one important point to mention in the case of work being sent abroad by post: it

115

pays to find out exactly what the postal regulations are. Sometimes it is cheaper to send the parcel as a 'small packet', particularly if you are sending it by airmail. This involves wrapping and tying it in a particular way. Also, make sure you get the right customs form in advance of posting. Large ones usually need to be attached to the parcel before adding the string.

6
'Look with Favour upon a Bold Beginning'

I can think of no better way of describing the purpose of this chapter than with those words by Virgil. Engraving is often a bold beginning.

But the bold beginnings I have in mind now are concerned with people: the engravers themselves. There are many interesting stories behind people's decisions to start upon new careers as engravers: how they became interested in the craft; how they started to work; what problems they encountered in the early stages; where they are now. Of course, most people who start upon engraving only want to engage in it for their own pleasure and as an absorbing craft for their leisure hours. It is the minority who make it a career. So I hope the majority, those who are looking for a fulfilling and creative occupation to be fitted in whenever possible to what may be limited free time, will find the following chapter both encouraging and interesting. More and more people are finding unimagined pleasure and interest in engraving and are discovering talents which they had no idea they possessed. For some this has meant the discovery of an unsuspected talent for drawing; others have found their greatest enjoyment of the work in developing their skills with electrical tools. Some, probably the minority, have had an art training and have found glass engraving a natural extension of their art work. But, leaving aside artistic talent or training, each engraver develops his or her own very individual style and approach to the work. The most important thing, I believe, is to know what final result you want to obtain. When you have this clearly in mind you will soon develop methods and skills which will enable you to achieve it.

Among contemporary engravers are some who have taken the

courageous step of leaving an established job in order to enter the adventurous world of the self-employed. Others have decided to make engraving a full-time second career upon retirement and have intentionally planned ahead for this. In some cases the idea of engraving did not occur until retirement had begun. Even though now established in the craft, not all would regard themselves as professionals, and, in any case, the dividing line between one who engraves for pleasure and a professional engraver cannot be defined if based on standards of work. Some engravers are fully professional in the commercial sense of the word and do indeed regard their work as their livelihood. But I think the greater number who engrave for profit would regard their work as providing an additional source of income only. Engravers are immensely varied in their approach to their work. Some, as well as finding the actual engraving very absorbing, also enjoy organising their work as a small business. Others really only want to engrave and shrink from the business side of things.

In compiling this chapter I have talked to a number of engravers in England and have corresponded at length with some in other countries. Almost all are members of the Guild of Glass Engravers. I have tried to give a picture of as many approaches to engraving as possible, by describing the situation and work of a cross-section of engravers. In many cases, as will be seen, engraving has led to other activities such as public speaking, teaching, and even opening a shop. It has been inevitable that only a small number of the total of either Guild members or of engravers working today could be included here (to have involved all would have more than filled another book!). I am very grateful for all the help, information and kindness they have so willingly given me, and I wish I could have written about many more. But I hope that what is told in the following pages will be an encouragement and inspiration to others and particularly to those who live far from places where they can meet other engravers. Those of us who are able to meet colleagues and exchange information and ideas, and see other people's work both historic and contemporary, do not always realise how fortunate we are. Art (and craft) really needs a meeting together of people in order to flourish. It is much harder to find inspiration only from within yourself and in isolation than for it to be sparked off by an exchange of thoughts and ideas with others.

So now to tell of some bold beginnings!

Even people who are no more than dimly aware of engraved glass have heard the name of Laurence Whistler. He and his work are now known the world over and his is the name instantly evoked by the words glass engraving.

His introduction to engraving was entirely by chance. At the age of twenty-two and just down from Balliol, his ambition was to be a poet and already two or three books of his poems had been published. That autumn he wrote a sonnet on the house of a friend in Northumberland, and as it was written to the house itself, it brought to his mind couplets and quatrains thought to have been written on window panes by Elizabethans and Jacobeans with diamond rings or diamond-tipped pencils. So he acquired a simple diamond tool of the type used in industry for writing on glass, and some suitable ink, and inscribed the poem on a sheet of glass to replace one in a first-floor window. That was the beginning of it all. More window-panes, with other verses, followed. Then, inevitably, he wished to engrave in the round and to use a variety of glass shapes. It was at this moment that he became conscious that here was an ancient craft, not a new one, which prompted him to search in books, galleries and showrooms for examples of work done in the seventeenth and eighteenth centuries in England and Holland. He soon realised that the craft was more or less defunct in England and that he was trying to revive it.

In fact, unknown to him, a young man of about his own age had also started to do some diamond point engraving in his spare time. This was W. J. Wilson, who in later years was chief designer and managing director of the Whitefriars Glass Company. Lawrence Whistler met him a year or so after he himself had started to engrave and it was only then that they discovered their shared interest in the craft. W. J. Wilson and David Peace were, at that time, the only people to take up the craft and the start of the great present-day revival of glass engraving in Britain is due solely to these three.

Since those early days Laurence Whistler has produced many engravings of international repute, often done on glass especially blown to his own design. His work is wide ranging, but much of it is pictorial – landscapes, buildings, moonlight, sunlight. And much of it springs from his thoughts and feelings as a poet. There are often meanings behind the engravings, sometimes obvious, but many have to be searched after. He has received many royal commissions and his work is in private collections and museums around the world. The books he has written about his engravings, and the beautiful photographs of his work which illustrate them, are an inspiration to all, whether engravers or not. When the Guild of Glass Engravers was founded in 1975, Laurence Whistler was elected its first president.

The story behind the reasons why Stephen Rickard became a glass engraver must surely be one of the most amazing of its kind. He had been trained as a sculptor at the Royal Academy Schools and was both teaching and exhibiting when, in 1953, he received a request from his elder brother in South Africa to find a piece of engraved glass to commemorate the Coronation. He duly searched London but could find nothing good enough to buy.

In the autumn of that year he went to visit his father in the Isle of Wight and while on the ferry he began to think about the mediocre engraved glass he had seen. If he could only find out how to mark glass he felt he could do better himself. *At the same time*, back at home, his wife, Lyn, was receiving an unexpected visit from her sister-in-law, undertaken for the express purpose of urging Lyn to go with her to see a friend who was a clairvoyant. Lyn's sister-in-law had felt that Stephen was depressed and something had impelled her to try to arrange this visit to the clairvoyant.

On meeting Lyn, the clairvoyant at once announced, 'I can't see anything about you; I can only see your husband,' and then went on to say that he would have an idea which would change his life. He would do something *like* his present work, but it would not be quite the same. He would meet many difficulties and would want to give up – but he must not. She added, reassuringly, that he would be very successful!

When Stephen returned from the Isle of Wight he was, of course, amazed to hear of the visit to the clairvoyant and, for his part, he was able to relate the good news that his father had been so interested in the idea of engraving that he had offered to buy the necessary tool for Stephen to begin work. Needless to say, that next day Stephen, too, visited the clairvoyant, who was again insistent that in spite of difficulties he would succeed in his new work – although she had no idea what this was to be.

So engraving began, first with a vibro tool. After a while, he longed to use other methods of work and at just the right moment met Reg Wilkinson, who knows *all* about glass. He suggested that Stephen might use diamond-impregnated wheels (used wet), suggested the shapes and sizes, and sold him an old pedal-operated dental drill. At that time, such wheels had to be specially made and the cost proved to be very high. So back again to the clairvoyant, who was quite firm that it was safe to order the wheels, adding, 'There is a hand being held out to you over water'. Holding up her right hand she said, 'I've got a little stick thing here with a wheel on the end of it, and there's pound notes spinning off it – does that make sense?' It did indeed make sense, though unfortunately it did not solve the problem of expensive tools. The next morning an air letter form from Stephen's brother in South Africa arrived containing a blank cheque and announcing that he was so pleased at the idea of engraving glass that Stephen might draw £100 on his account to buy equipment. In 1953, £100 was a great deal of money. Since then, success has indeed come and Stephen Rickard's beautiful drill engravings are renowned.

Elly Eliades, much to her surprise, has become a central point in the ever-expanding world of hand-engraved glass in Britain.

She and her husband, Socrates, are Greek and have lived in London for many years. Elly had led an active life as a mother of three daughters and the wife of a businessman, yet always felt that she was not using her time creatively enough. A period of poor health left her feeling severely depressed and in an attempt to cure this she attended several adult education courses in a variety of subjects, none of which she found made sufficient demands upon her. One final effort to find something creative was when she joined a class on glass decorating at Isleworth Polytechnic. Part of the course was on engraving and while attending classes, Elly saw a particular piece of engraved glass which instantly made her feel that here was the end of her search for self-expression: she would engrave glass.

After a while, an unexpected event led on to what was to prove an important influence in her life – and it is not too much to say that many other people eventually benefited greatly from it. The polytechnic was asked to provide some glassblowers and engravers to demonstrate their craft at a large London exhibition and she found herself demonstrating engraving. Soon she was surprised to find that Ronald Stennett-Willson, the author of *The Beauty of Modern*

121

Glass, was watching her at work and was asking for a photograph of some of her engravings for his book. She modestly tried to refer him to an official source which would provide photographs of professional work – a craft society or guild, perhaps. And then she discovered that glass engravers had no such guild. Elly's demonstration work was also seen by someone who was at that time unknown to her, Elaine Freed. It interested her and she, too, joined the engraving class at the polytechnic. This proved to be the final link in the chain. Elly and Elaine realised that their interests in glass engraving were alike. They wanted to broaden their horizons, learn more about the craft, meet other engravers. In talking together they noted that there was no co-ordination of engravers in Britain, no guild or society, no central point of reference. So, with invaluable help and support from their husbands, they decided, just the two of them, to organise the formation of a Guild of Glass Engravers. More has been told of the workings of the Guild in Chapter 1 but it is fitting to say here that its existence has been a big influence in the lives of a number of people; it has given purpose to their work and has been a source of inspiration. Above all, it has certainly been the mainspring of the vigorous revival of hand-engraved glass which is taking place in Britain today.

Since the formation of the Guild, Elaine Freed has continued to work very actively as honorary secretary but regards her engraving as a spare-time interest. Elly Eliades, on the other hand, has made engraving her major interest. The Guild, she feels, is her life and she works indefatigably as honorary membership secretary. But engraving has led her on to other interests, as it has so many others. She now teaches and lectures on the subject, and is the perfect example of going out to get what you want. She felt she would like to contribute to a craft she loves by teaching others – perhaps two or three people on a voluntary basis. But where could she find students? On the spur of the moment she walked into her local police station (of all places!) and asked how she could find people to teach. A puzzled policeman suggested asking the adult education centre next door. She instantly did so, and after initial amazement on their part she was offered a class of thirty students, not three. In addition to teaching and lecturing, she concentrates on experimental engraving for her own pleasure, accepting special commissions from time to time. Her husband, although not an engraver, is now vice-president of the Guild, and her eldest daughter, Katia, also engraves. It seems like a modern version of the sociable groups who met together in seventeenth century Holland to practise their engraving, although in this case it is nearly a whole family!

Tim Appleyard is another engraver who left an established career – as a schoolmaster at a boys' school – in order to engrave professionally. Some years ago, wishing to help raise money for his local church, he hit upon the idea of putting a design of the church on to some glasses and trying to sell these at the church fête. He was not then an engraver and knew nothing about the craft. However, he possessed a Burgess Hobbyist Engraver and made a simple design, using the tool literally to draw on the glass. He worked on very cheap glasses and priced each one (modestly!) at 40p, including engraving.

The results were amazing. Even before the fête opened Tim had received enough orders for these glasses to show a profit of £80. By the end of the fête he had orders which would show a profit of £120. So he had a very busy time during the school summer holiday, working through all his orders. By the time all these were finished, the standard of his work had, understandably, greatly improved and he found people kept on coming back with more orders. He began making his own hand tools, mounting diamond tips in felt-pen holders, and for the next four years he worked exclusively with these and with a Burgess Engraver, exploring every possible way of working with them. By the end of that time he could regard his engraving as a paying spare-time occupation.

At that point, domestic circumstances made it necessary for him to work at home, and engraving was the answer. So he gave up his teaching job and became a full-time engraver. It was a big decision to make.

Tim worked from home for the next year, not only engraving in his studio but also taking his work round the country to many craft fairs and similar exhibitions. He did not, however, find this very advantageous. It involved a great deal of expensive travel; a lot of bulky equipment, such as display cabinets, tables and so on, had to be taken along each time; his work was not exhibited to advantage; and above all it involved much packing and unpacking of glass, with all its attendant hazards.

After this first year, his domestic situation stabilised, and he decided he was not getting sufficient commissions to make engraving a viable long-term occupation. He knew he needed to reach a wider public, but he also wished to stop attending craft shows and thus avoid all the problems of constantly having to transport a highly breakable commodity. So his next big decision was to take a small shop in nearby Arundel.

This proved to be the turning point. An attractive display of Tim's own engraved glass is exhibited there in an ideal setting: display cabinets, in just the right dim surroundings, have fluorescent lighting to illuminate the glass. Visitors may buy from this, or they may commission their own choice of design. In addition to producing and selling engraved glass, Tim was built up a range of unengraved high-quality glassware. He has found this an advantageous move. Not only can customers choose their own particular glass and then commission the engraving they want done on it, but other engravers can find unusual blanks on which to do their own work.

After eighteen months in the shop, Tim now feels that he has successfully established the kind of business which suits him personally, and that he can now look forward to a second career as a glass engraver.

Anne Cotton, who now engraves professionally, was originally trained as a book illustrator, specialising in wood engraving. Perhaps this eventual progression to glass engraving was a natural development because, when she was a child, her father, a retired naval officer, had taught her aquatint etching. Although at that time glass engraving simply did not enter her world, she feels that her early experience of other engraving techniques prepared her, even if subconsciously, for her work with glass in later years. As she puts it, 'Something comes from the appreciation of tone value; aquatint etching grounded me in the relationship of flat tones.' She feels, too, that her art training was directed towards linear work, especially black and white. This, though unknown to her at the time, had particular relevance with regard to the future.

When her art training ended, Anne diverted into totally different paths and trained as a church worker. After training, the work was very varied and for some years it had an educational connexion which provided an opportunity for her to specialise in visual aids. It was a strenuous life, dealing often with human crises of one sort or another. She feels all this taught her to think analytically, which has proved invaluable in her work as an engraver.

Anne's introduction to hand-engraved glass came entirely by accident. A friend came by chance upon Laurence Whistler's book *Initials in the Heart* and thought it looked interesting and different; just the kind of thing which would interest Anne. Naturally, it did and from then on, with a new awareness of engraved glass, Anne sought out more of Laurence Whistler's books and tracked down exhibitions of his work.

Then, slowly, everything fell into place. A tungsten carbide tool, advertised as 'capable of writing on anything', was acquired, and during the next ten years she did a handful of engravings. Then, because of a depressive illness, she had to give up her job. In due course, with time to do so, she turned to things which pleased her: first painting, then back to engraving. A landmark at this point was joining the Guild of Glass Engravers and sharing in its first exhibition at Isleworth.

That was the beginning of a new career as a glass engraver. She saved the money to buy a drill and this became her usual method of work, though stipple engraving takes second place only because it is too slow for a freelance depending upon the income for her engraving. Anne is wholly self-taught and experiments constantly with different glass shapes and different tools and techniques. She feels that you can be taught most techniques and to think about engraving subjects and treatment, but that it may be an advantage to work alone since an individual style is for each engraver to discover and develop. It grows, she feels, from personal temperament, experiences and feelings, and is the result of deliberate choices of ways in which to express these by careful skill of hand.

Anne exhibits frequently and works to commissions of all kinds, preferring non-functional glass and subjects that are 'about something', often starting from natural objects or things seen and working towards abstractions and, in particular, the expression of Christian ideas.

Among contemporary engravers, there is at least one who is, it could be said, in a world apart. Sister Giles is a nun in the Order of Poor Clares at Arundel in Sussex, and there must be very few nuns in the world who are glass engravers. Some engravers in Britain, and indeed in other countries, have only rare opportunities of seeing any engraved glass, but at least in theory the possibility exists. For Sister Giles it does not: the Poor Clares are an enclosed order.

Bearing in mind, then, that Sister Giles does not leave the convent, how did she ever become aware of the craft, let alone embark upon learning it? She was always resourceful and used to varying occupations. Before entering the convent she had been an actress; her work in the convent had been to undertake printing at a professional level, and after many years of producing a considerable amount of printed material and undertaking many commercial orders on behalf of the convent, she changed over to supervising the designing of vestments. So by temperament she was ready for new challenges.

The beginning of the new craft of engraving was in 1965 when a friend got her a book from the local public library: Laurence Whistler's *Initials in the Heart*. She was at once fascinated by the photographs of his own engravings which illustrated the book. She wanted to try to do this work but doubted if this would be possible for anyone in her situation. Her practical solution to this was to write to Laurence Whistler himself and ask, simply, 'Can I do this work in a convent?' His response was immediately encouraging. He thought she could, and gave her helpful information on types of glass and methods of engraving. Above all, he sent her a diamond tool which he had made and used himself.

So Sister Giles started to engrave. At first, her designs were simple patterns of flowers and birds. The time she could spend on the work was limited and it was difficult to get glass to work on because she could not go out to look around and buy any. So for the next four years her work was very small in quantity.

However, in 1972 things developed rapidly and in a totally unexpected way. There was an amalgamation between the Arundel Community and one that was founded in Prinzenhof in Belgium in 1621. In the course of building work resulting from this, the chapel at Arundel underwent some reconstruction and new windows were needed. At the same time, someone connected with the convent asked if these new windows could be designed to commemorate his son. Stained glass was first suggested and at this point, quite out of the blue, Sister Giles suddenly found herself asking, 'Can I engrave the windows?' Astonishing – because she had never seen any engraved windows and had no idea how to do them.

The resulting task was indeed daunting. She was soon faced with three panels of 5mm (¼in) plate glass, 1.8m (6ft) high and 45cm

(1½ft) wide, and her sole experience of engraving was a few tentative efforts on small glasses with a delicate tool – and apart from the original tool in her collection which Laurence Whistler had given her, she had had to resort to making her own, using tiny diamond chips and mounting them in penholders with sealing-wax. So she once again asked Laurence Whistler for advice. Trying to engrave these windows by stippling would be like trying to paint the ceiling of the Sistine Chapel with a water-colour brush, he said, and advised her to buy a flexible drive drill. So, by stages, Sister Giles got in touch with a supplier and acquired the drill and some burrs and wheels. Every step of the way was undertaken, really, as an act of faith. She had no knowledge of even such basic things as transferring the design on to the glass, let alone how to use a drill or what kinds of burrs were needed. However, she drew the design to a smaller size than the windows, using paper, and then enlarged this basic drawing. Carbon paper was used for tracing the design on to the glass, and so the engraving was begun.

The windows, which are now mounted in the convent chapel, are illustrated in plate 40. They are displayed not against daylight but against a black background and are illuminated by side lighting with fluorescent strips. Their beauty cannot be described, nor can it be captured by a photograph. They were designed as a double commemoration: the left-hand and right-hand windows commemorate the amalgamation of the two communities, Prinzenhof and Arundel, and the centre window is a memorial. Sister Giles' next work is to engrave another commemorative panel for the chapel. She undertakes occasional commissions but the amount of work she can do is governed by her commitments in the convent.

The importance of her work, I feel, is that she has shown that engraving is compatible with an enclosed life. Could her engraving, perhaps, be the start of a new kind of work done in convents? In the past, nuns have been renowned for embroidery, fine needlework, illumination, and many kindred skilled handicrafts. Now, as the demand for these lessens, can one dream of glass engraving spreading through convents the world over?

Peter Pullan, by contrast, has made engraving a very successful and fulfilling second career. He is a retired RAF officer and deliberately planned to make it a full-time occupation upon his retirement. Some time before this took place, he saw some engraved glass

PLATES

Plate 42 Cullet by Majella Taylor; engraved with diamond wheels and polished

Plate 43 Drill engraving by Denis Bustard

Plate 44 Engraved with Burgess Engraver by Pat Robinson

Plate 45 Drill engraving by Ann Dybka – two cylinders, one inside the other *(Ian Provest)*

Plate 46 Doors of Stapleford Church, engraved by David Peace

Plate 47 Diamond point stipple engraving by Eric Smith *(Raymond Fortt)*

Plate 48 Stipple engraving by Peter David

Plate 49 Stipple and line engraving by Roy James

Plate 50 Drill engraving by Ed Brantley *(Jolynn Orr)*

Plate 51 Panel engraved by Peter Weinrich

Plate 52 Church window by Marlene Frothinger. Drill engraving combined with stained glass and designed to be seen against a background of the trees outside

Plate 53 Engraved by Bill Harman using diamond point and tungsten carbide

Plate 54 Egyptian glass with combed decoration, sixth century BC *Crown Copyright. Victoria and Albert Museum*

Plate 55 Venetian wineglass sixteenth or seventeenth century *Crown Copyright. Victoria and Albert Museum*

Plate 56 Venetian 'tazza', second half of sixteenth century *Crown Copyright. Victoria and Albert Museum*

Plate 57 Venetian wineglass with latticinio decoration. Early seventeenth century *Crown Copyright. Victoria and Albert Museum*

Plate 58 German or Netherlandish green glass 'Roemer' with 32 prunts, c1600 *Crown Copyright. Victoria and Albert Museum*

Plate 59 English glass, diamond engraved with the arms of Butler Buggin, 1676 *Crown Copyright. Victoria and Albert Museum*

42

44

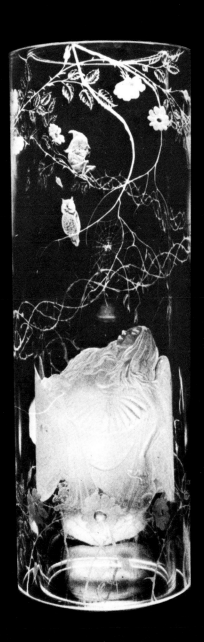

45

In thy sight
a thousand
years are as
yesterday

They are like
a dream at
daybreak
AD MCMLXX

46

48

do not wait for the last judgement, it happens every day. ALBERT CAMUS

54

58

59

in museums, as well as in a television programme about engraving, which had greatly interested him. What finally led to his taking it up himself was seeing an advertisement for a Burgess Engraver. This means of engraving appealed to him and this is the tool he has used ever since.

Having acquired a Burgess engraving tool and done a few tentative engravings, there followed, at just the right moment, two events which were a great assistance and a great influence. The first was his discovery of the then newly formed Guild of Glass Engravers. This fortunately coincided with an RAF duty visit to London, which enabled him to visit the Guild's headquarters and obtain much useful information. The second event was the Guild's exhibition at Isleworth, the first it had ever undertaken. Peter Pullan was among many who were inspired by this wonderful collection of engraved glass by Guild members.

So, equipped with the tool of his choice, and fortified by the recollection of the Guild's exhibition. Peter Pullan started off on another career. At first, and entirely self-taught, he went to work at the dining-room table. As he progressed he built himself a well-equipped studio and painstakingly explored every possible method of using the Burgess Engraver. He specialised in lettering and heraldry – particularly Service badges on which he is an expert – and has developed a very personal style of engraving. In his hands the Burgess Engraver produces anything from the most delicate stippling to the densest matting. He has evolved a method of drawing to suit his specialised requirements. A preliminary drawing is made on graph paper, usually redrawn and repeatedly erased until the precise requirement is achieved. Finally, it is traced on to the glass.

All his lettering, mainly based on reference books, is first drawn on to graph paper and then traced on to the glass. About half his heraldic work is copied from designs given to him by customers; the rest he draws himself. Other designs, such as Service badges, aircraft and animals, are based on photographs.

Peter Pullan runs his engraving career as a successful business, which is what he intended it to be. As well as working on engraving in his studio, he has also lectured on the subject to Service Officers' courses.

Majella Taylor's reasons for starting work on engraving glass were simple: she liked drawing as opposed to painting, and wanted to draw on something more permanent than paper. She saw John Hutton's magnificent engraved windows in Coventry Cathedral and decided that glass must be her medium. At that point she noticed an advertisement for a Burgess engraving tool, bought one, and started to engrave pictures on ordinary window glass. She worked in this way for about three years and found a market for her work, mainly selling in local shops.

At the end of three years she felt ready to try more tools and to develop a different technique. So she bought a flexible drive drill and some small diamond wheels and experimented with cutting deeply into the glass and then polishing in various ways. Everything was self-taught and experimental and she had still seen no other hand-engraved glass.

Always eager for more work and greater challenges, Majella applied to West Dean College to start a series of short residential courses in engraved glass. After showing her work, she was at once appointed as tutor and has now taught at West Dean for about six years. She continued constantly to experiment with more tools and more methods, and found that her earlier art training as a fabric designer was a help. However, she recalls that at the beginning of her own work on engraving it was difficult to translate her ideas, which at that time tended to spring from fabric design, into working in such a different medium.

Her output of engraving is very considerable. She always enjoys experimenting with new techniques and new materials and feels that glass as a medium offers great possibilities. At present, she is exploring the use of colour combined with engraving, for which she plans to use some stained glass techniques.

Majella Taylor has always been very single-minded and determined about her engraving. For her, engraving on glass has meant an extremely busy, interesting and entirely successful career and – an important consideration – one which can be combined with running a home and bringing up a family.

By contrast, Denis Bustard is among those for whom engraving has provided a very busy second career upon retirement. He came across engraved glass entirely by chance. His working life had been spent with a large airline and, like so many others in a similar situation, he began to wonder how to occupy his retirement in a way which would be interesting in its own right and which could also be run as small business enterprise. He felt this would provide the right amount of incentive and that it would be an added interest and challenge. Above all, he wanted to do something which would involve using his hands and his mind. So the choice was – clockmaking. 'So many people retire', he says, 'and then just work at some craft on a casual basis. I wanted some motivation.'

But before he could start on clockmaking he was given a presentation in recognition of some work he had done for a committee. This changed his life: the presentation was a piece of engraved glass. Denis says, with some surprise, that although he supposes he must have seen a lot of engraved glass around before, this was the first time he had actually *looked* at any. The result of looking was that he suddenly thought 'this is what I want to do', and with great determination he set off on this new path. He chose a flexible drive drill and diamond dental burrs as his tools, and is entirely self-taught.

That was five years ago at the time of writing. His thoughts about his work and the style he has developed will, I hope, give encouragement to many others similarly placed. He insists that he is not 'artistic' but that he regards himself as a craftsman. He does not seek to create designs but concentrates on heraldry, architectural subjects and meticulously executed lettering. He uses Letraset for his lettering and engraves in a plain, unornamented style – no flowing calligraphic designs. For heraldry he is provided with the designs, and for architectural subjects he uses photographs. Many of these he takes himself. He has evolved a style of work which is very distinctive because it is so accurate and clear. His mechanical bent has enabled him to equip his studio with many highly ingenious gadgets, which are useful and labour-saving. As a beginner, his greatest technical problem was learning to think in terms of light, not shade – of having to lighten the light areas of a design and not shade in the dark parts. He overcame this by making working drawings beforehand on black paper with a white pencil. Another problem was where to buy tools, which is why I have included a list of suppliers in the Appendix (see page 181).

Denis has built up an enjoyable life round his work as an engraver, not only practising the craft, but also being in demand as a speaker on the subject. This in turn has led to even more commissions. He also derives great pleasure from helping beginners. He has no desire to teach in the formal sense of the word but enjoys spending half a day with one person at a time 'just to get them started' as he puts it. He feels that one of the greatest rewards engraving has brought him has been the many interesting and friendly people he has met in the course of his work.

Pat Robinson would be the first to agree that her reasons for deciding to engrave glass were rather different from most other people's. She was looking for some way of being remembered: she wanted to leave her mark. (And what more appropriate way of doing so than on a piece of glass!) It all happened, as in so many other cases, entirely by accident. She attended a talk and demonstration by an engraver and at the conclusion of this, some tools were available for inspection and trial. Pat picked up a drill, wrote her name on a goblet and could have sold it then and there. She knew immediately that this was what she had been looking for.

She started by simply engraving Gothic lettering on cheap glasses. She was fortunate in two ways, though. She not only had a specialist knowledge of an alphabet which happened in itself to be decorative, but her earlier work as a draughtswoman enabled her to place her lettering unerringly on the glass with no need to measure. She more or less just picked up her Burgess tool and wrote on the glass – very quickly. At first she worked just for her own pleasure with no thought of the financial side – at least just for a week or two, she says! Then, as she puts it, everything was decided by public demand. She found there was a constant demand for cheap glasses with some lettering engraved upon them at speed and priced modestly. Her work is in complete contrast with that of most other engravers in that it does not aim to be a considered as art. She has added to her lettering simple engraved 'drawings' of local buildings or well-known historical figures, and deliberately keeps her work quick and uncomplicated. This, combined with the fact that she mainly works on a cheaper range of glasses, has enabled her to keep her prices low and to work for a different market. But the glass she uses is all carefully chosen for its pleasing shape. Alongside this type of work she accepts commissions for more elaborate work in a higher price range, and engraves windows for houses in her area. She has already taken part in an exhibition in France and plans to expand into other markets. Her work is lively and spontaneous and she finds there is a great demand for glasses with initials and dates to commemorate family events. She is an immensely busy engraver.

In her case, too, engraving has led on to something else. Two years ago she was asked to give a talk about her work to a charity meeting. She had never spoken in public before and was much alarmed at the idea. However, she agreed to speak and painstakingly went to work to write out her lecture. After writing, as she thought, at length, she read out her text and found it occupied just five minutes! So in desperation, she simply took along a few notes and hoped for the best. And the best was very good indeed. Since then she had been in constant demand as a speaker, with engagements stretching a year ahead.

Lest it be thought that there is no half-way between doing a little engraving in some spare time and being a full-time engraver to professional standards of excellence, there are many people who manage to combine a firm position in the world of engraving with a very demanding career in some totally unrelated field – or one which at first sight appears so. Among them are David Peace, an architect town-planner in Staffordshire and Cambridgeshire for over thirty years, Eric Smith who is a doctor and Peter David who is an oceanographer.

David Peace, who wrote the foreword to this book, has no idea why he first bought a diamond pencil; all he remembers is that in 1935 he engraved a monogram on a goblet as a present for a sister. A family wedding present was engraved in 1936, then little more until after the war. At that time, his wife reminded him of his early engraving and suggested an engraved goblet as a present to the family doctor for his care of the family. David Peace then thought of engraving with a diamond drill and asked advice from his dentist. He spent what he describes as 'a useful evening' at the dentist's surgery 'engraving on the only glass available – dentists' spit mugs!' Soon after that the doctor's goblet was engraved with the words *Homines ad deos nulla re propius accedunt quam salutem hominibus dando* (Men approach the gods in nothing so much as in giving health to men), which is surely a tremendous undertaking for an early engraving on a goblet!

The next landmark was reading an anonymous advertisement in *The Times* asking for suggestions for a golden wedding present. David Peace replied in a way which not only expresses his own views on engraved glass but also gets to the heart of the matter. His reply was, 'Something personal, usable, decorative, specially made and ready on time – in short – an engraved goblet.' Of course he was commissioned to engrave the goblet and, he says, since then there has never been a dull moment and rarely an idle one.

Most of his work, now widely known, incorporates lettering or heraldry or both. Lettering has been a lifelong interest and in many instances he has used it to form a complete design round a goblet or bowl. As an architect and planner he is always concerned with the right relationship of buildings to a site, and thus regards his engraving as a logical extension of this aim – the closest kinship of the engraved design and the shape of the glass.

David Peace clearly believes in practising what he preaches. He was approached with a suggestion that he should engrave windows for the Lady Chapel in Manchester Cathedral which was being rebuilt after wartime bombing. Ten windows were needed – to be designed, engraved and fixed, all in a month! (Engraved glass: '. . . decorative, specially made and ready on time . . .') So he took on the task, describing it as a 'a few panes a day, sent in parcels for leading up regularly, and so it was done'.

Since then there have been many windows, and even doors. Much has been engraved in situ, like the doors of Stapleford Church done in 1975 and illustrated in plate 46. In addition to these, he has worked on a great variety of glass shapes: goblets, decanters, bowls, trophies, obelisks, carboys, even a one-inch thick slab of Sydney Opera House glass, an hour-glass, and a radiometer. He also found time to be the first chairman of the Guild of Glass Engravers, holding the office for five years and subsequently becoming its President.

Eric Smith is a doctor – it is hardly necessary to say a busy one, they all are – who manages to make engraving a very fulfilling secondary occupation. He used to paint but became discouraged and felt there was a limit to what he could achieve. But apart from a wish to be involved with some kind of visual art, he also liked working with his hands, and engraving glass provided just that.

He, too, is self-taught and began with the simplest writing diamond. In the early days of his engraving, he explored all methods of working with hand tools and built up a small stock of diamond and tungsten carbide tools with different points. He clearly enjoys stippling and much of his work is carried out using this method. An example of this is illustrated in plate 47, and an added point of interest in this subject is that the design was made from one of his own photographs. Returning by car from a holiday, he suddenly glimpsed a windmill and thought it might be a possible subject for an engraving. He took a photograph and the design was built up from that chance view. Because engraving can, in many instances, be managed with only a few tools and no workshop, he often takes a piece of glass and some tools when going away on holiday and finds engraving a great relaxation.

Eric Smith now uses a flexible drive drill as well as hand tools, sometimes working with the drill on its own and sometimes combining both methods. He receives as many commissions as he can undertake, bearing in mind the demanding nature of his work as a doctor, and exhibits regularly in London and Paris. In the distant days of retirement he plans to be a full-time engraver.

Peter David: oceanographer and glass engraver. Surely the only stipple engraver to work at this delicate craft while at sea? (It is best to choose calm weather, he says).

Peter David's professional work has involved not only leading a very busy life on land, but also spending frequent periods at sea, researching into marine life. Alongside this, he has built up a parallel career as a glass engraver.

He first became aware of stipple engraving during one of his periods at sea. On board were several magazines and he happened to pick up one which contained a picture of an engraving by Laurence Whistler with some description of how this work was done. Peter was instantly interested in this but did not follow it up because it looked so impossible to do. A long time afterwards, he was looking through a publisher's catalogue and saw mention of a book about glass engraving. He got the book (it happened to be my own) and thought this was something he might be able to do.

So, with no more guidance than the book, he began to engrave. His first attempt was, he says, not quite bad enough to prevent his continuing. So on he went – and it is fortunate that he did. His chosen method of work is stipple engraving and he has now brought this to a peak of perfection. It is the most delicate, and the most beautiful, imaginable work.

Peter David now has a well-established reputation as a stipple engraver in addition to his professional life as an oceanographer, and he accepts commissions. In the future, when he retires, he plans to continue and expand his work as an engraver.

Hand engraving on glass is also reviving to some extent overseas, if in a limited way at the moment. The Guild of Glass Engravers has overseas members, both lay and craft, and engravers in the USA and Australia, in particular, are doing some interesting work. They are few in number, but everything must have a beginning. What sets these overseas engravers apart from their British colleagues is their isolation from the mainstream of the craft. Hardly any of them has ever seen any hand-engraved glass nor have they seen any tools. They do not meet other engravers; they have nowhere to go for help in their work and no one with whom to exchange ideas. All of them are, of necessity, self-taught. They are inventive and are continually experimenting with new ways of using their tools. They are the real pioneers.

An engraver whom this description fits very well is Roy James who lives in Smyrna, Delaware, USA. He started to engrave because he likes to experiment with new things. His work with machinery had given him experience of working with tungsten carbide and it occurred to him that if tungsten was made into sharp points, it could be used to engrave glass. So he designed and made his own tools, which he still does although nowadays he uses them in conjunction with manufactured tools. All this was back in 1957 and Roy has been engraving ever since – still without having seen any other hand-engraved glass. He uses inexpensive glass and works on whatever shapes he has access to. He usually engraves for his own interest and pleasure, but does sometimes accept commissions. A piece of his work is illustrated in plate 49.

Ed Brantley, living in Los Angeles, is a good example of patience and determination over a long period. His interest in decorated glass goes back to childhood days when, as a little boy living in a community on the East Side of Los Angeles, he used to watch plate glass being sandblasted. The glass was then used as panels in front doors, and he recalls his vivid pleasure in walking with his grandmother to visit her friends because each front door was different!

Many years later, while serving in the US Airforce, he saw instruction being given on how to engrave on plastic and this, too, greatly interested him. But he was never able to get the right tools for the work. Nearly twenty-five years went by and finally he bought some engraving equipment and began to experiment on plastic, teaching himself. From plastic he turned to glass, at first using cheap domestic soda glass, even wine bottles. The next step was working on lead crystal, experimenting all the time. He did not see any engraved glass: all he had for guidance were such photographs as he could find in books at his local library. Now, ten years later, he has evolved his own method of working with a dental drill and diamond and carborundum burrs. He does all his engraving under a water drip. It has taken many years to reach the stage where he is now a full-time engraver, working to commissions from many quarters, but he has done so by sheer perserverance.

Don Sharp of Amarillo, Texas, is another American who is very interested in glass engraving – to use his own words. But it has to be solely for his own pleasure at the moment as he is fully occupied in running his own stained glass studio. He uses engraving in an unusual way, working on pieces of flat glass and combining these with pieces of stained glass to make hangings. He is self-taught and finds the combination of the two crafts – stained glass and engraved glass – go well together.

Jeffrey W. Clark of Stanhope, New Jersey, is a singer who discovered glass engraving by chance. Between singing engagements, and therefore with little money to do Christmas shopping, he noticed some photo glass which had been thrown away. It occurred to him that he might use his talent for sketching to do something on the glass. By experimenting with a tungsten carbide tip, he discovered he could engrave on the glass and went on to produce engraved pictures. These were backed with black velvet and framed with wood, and became welcome Christmas presents. He became increasingly interested in the craft and began to engrave on curved shapes as well as flat glass. His method is to work out his designs first and then to draw them on the glass with Indian ink, finally engraving with diamond tools. He now engraves on a great variety of glass shapes and uses flat glass for pictures and mirrors. He also uses flat glass for panels which are mounted on wooden blocks and illuminated from the base. He works at his engraving in parallel with his career as a singer, feeling that too many years of study and hard work have gone into singing for it to be abandoned now.

One of the few engravers in Canada is Peter Weinrich, who happens to be executive director of the Canadian Crafts Council. His interest in engraving goes back a long time and he can hardly pinpoint exactly what started it. But, as with many other people, a series

153

of small incidents – such as reading about Laurence Whistler and his work, seeing one of his engravings, buying an engraved goblet as a present for his father – eventually led to a wish to start engraving. He searched out all that could be found about engraving in the library, bought a tungsten carbide tool and – self-taught – started to work. His greatest problem was, and still is, the great difficulty in getting any undecorated lead crystal upon which he can work. However, he was extremely resourceful and, realising the problem of getting crystal, made good use of what was at hand in the way of flat glass. A supply of this in the form of offcuts was very conveniently available at his local glass shop which, as Peter Weinrich puts it, 'chucks them out into a large bin at the back from whence they can be picked up free'!

He finds flat glass a good base for lettering and the photograph of the panel (plate 51) is the first piece of glass he ever engraved, with the exception of a single letter tried out separately. That first piece of work taught him a lot, mainly about the amount of pressure required when using an engraving tool. He had thought the glass should be attacked furiously and by so doing made rough splintered lines for the infilling of the lettering. In fact, this was exactly the effect he had wanted to produce for this kind of lettering, but it had been fortuitous. He plans to do more lettering on flat glass before moving on to curved surfaces.

Another Canadian-based engraver who works in considerable isolation from the craft point of view is Marlene Frothinger, an American who now lives in Nova Scotia. She had always appreciated glass as a material so it was perhaps not surprising that she became involved with it. She had seen mainly acid-etched and stained glass and her first work with glass was to produce acid-etched Christmas tree decorations. The scope of this work increased to include boxes, lampshades, panels and windows. She read everything she could find about glass and thus became aware of engraved glass although she had never seen any. So, entirely self-taught, she moved on to engraving. Because she finds it so difficult to get crystal shapes she, too, engraves on flat glass. These engravings are mounted as windows, often in conjuction with stained glass. Another use for engravings on small pieces of flat glass is as lids for boxes made of stained glass.

Marlene Frothinger is busy with her work on etched glass but her

154

intention is to devote an increasing amount of time to engraving. 'Art', she says, 'is an expression of what is happening here and now, and diamond point engraving is the purest and most beautiful art form to me.' A sentiment many would share.

In Australia, too, glass engraving is just beginning. One engraver who has worked mainly for his pleasure in the craft is Nicholas Draffin, who lives in Sydney. He, like others, was first attracted to engraving when he read a book about Laurence Whistler's work. He concentrated on diamond point engraving and found that his greatest enjoyment came from engraving small, personal presents. Two other Australian engravers, living far apart and working professionally, are Anne Dybka who lives and works in North Sydney, and Bill Harman who lives in Queensland. Anne Dybka had a background in glass, having been a glass designer for several years. This brought her into contact with copper wheel engraving but she had no experience of work done with either a diamond point or a drill. However, she wished to experiment with these different techniques and simply taught herself. At first she engraved large-scale architectural work, but now usually works on a smaller scale. She displays much of her work with illumination – for example, large cullets have tiny holes drilled in the base so that small lights may be inserted, panels and cylinders are illuminated from the base. Among the larger of her works are two cast panels of 25mm (1in) thick glass in the foyer of a bank, and she has also engraved thick glass doors. Anne Dybka is a busy professional engraver who has had many major commissions and several exhibitions. She now has her own workshop in an arts centre complex in the Argyle Arts Centre in the old 'Rocks' area of Sydney, and works exclusively on engraving. Examples of her work can be seen in plates 21 and 45.

Bill Harman first became interested in glass engraving when he read an illustrated article by Laurence Whistler in 1951. At about the same time, he bought a copy of *A Manual on Etching and Engraving Glass* by G. M. Heddle and found some of the illustrations in this a great inspiration. The next step was to buy a diamond tool and try to engrave a *bottle*! 'After about half an hour the chip of diamond fell off', he says. It was asking rather a lot of a diamond (though I don't forget that I, too, badly damaged my first diamond tool – but not on a bottle). He was a meterologist, and for various reasons there was no more engraving for the next ten years. But, as so many people

155

find, it is very difficult to drive engraving entirely from your mind once your interest has been aroused. So when he had more time at his disposal, he again became involved with engraving. This time he bought some thin tungsten carbide cylinders and designed and made his own tools. He started by engraving a few goblets as presents. Then there was another long gap – eleven years this time – until 1978. In that year he engraved a goblet as a wedding present, and when the large department store in Brisbane from whom he bought the goblet heard that he wanted to engrave it, they asked to see the finished work. This was the turning point. He was asked to demonstrate diamond point engraving in the glass department of the store, and in three days received ten commissions. Others have followed. He engraves a wide range of subjects – heraldic designs, ships, aeroplanes, animals – using both tungsten carbide and diamond point tools. Heraldry he finds very demanding, particularly as the designs frequently have to be redrawn to the required size. For this purpose, he has made himself a pantograph and finds this extremely helpful. He sharpens all his own tungsten points on a diamond lap, revolving it with a small electric motor.

Bill Harman, too, is now a professional engraver, and greatly enjoys his work. For him too engraving has formed a satisfying and useful second career during his retirement from a first career.

7
The Development of Glass

When embarking on any craft it is both interesting and useful to know as much as possible about the materials with which you are working, and glass is such a fascinating material that I hope it will add to your enjoyment of engraving to know something about how glassmaking developed through the ages and how it is produced now.

I sometimes wonder if there is anything we take so much for granted as glass. One could speculate endlessly on which particular discoveries have had the greatest influence upon everyday life. The wheel at once comes to mind, but surely glass must be high on the list. Imagine life without it. The world would indeed be dark – or, at least, it would have been dark for a very long time. At this point in the twentieth century, I suppose we would all have been supplied with windows made of some alternative material, but for many centuries people would have lived very dimly indeed. So it is natural to associate glass with light (and engraving is closely associated with light too). But it is not only the use of glass in windows we take for granted: the world is full of glass used in a multitude of ways which no longer cause a moment's wonder or appreciation. Containers, mirrors, protective coverings, cooking utensils, industrial uses – the list is long. The fragile material can be toughened so that it is heatproof, flameproof, shatterproof and bulletproof.

Throughout its long history glass has been used both for decoration and in the making of vessels of all kinds intended for daily use. In ancient times, colour was an important element in the decorative use of glass and, in any case, the method of making clear, colourless glass was not yet known. Later on, various applied decorations were added, such as engraving, painting and gilding. In churches, coloured glass was used to make windows which were in themselves decorative. But that is moving ahead a long way from the first appearance of glass. How did it appear? And where?

It would be very satisfactory to be able to give exact details of the discovery of glass but unfortunately these have been lost during the thousands of years which have elapsed. Pliny gave an account of it and although this may be partly true, it is not accepted as fact. Pliny lived in the first century AD and the oldest glass yet found is in the form of small beads dating back to about 2,000 BC, so rather a large gap in time divided Pliny from ancient Egyptian glass. However, in his account of the discovery of glass he tells how some Phoenician merchants, travelling between Egypt and Syria, landed at the mouth of the River Belus and encamped for the night. They lit a fire and used some of their cargo (which was blocks of natron) to support their cooking pots. In the morning the merchants found that the natron, which is a form of soda, had fused with the sandy base beneath it to form a kind of glass. If this really happened the glass so formed would have been soluble in water – 'water glass' as we know it. However, sand and soda are indeed two of the basic constituents of glass, so if the fire had been extremely hot this fusion could perhaps have taken place. In due course, another ingredient, lime, was added in order to make a durable material.

Whatever its origins, glass is a very ancient material. Even before the first glass beads of 2,000 BC there were ceramic beads which were given a glaze made of a glass-like substance. Then came the stage when glass was worked as an independent material, first being made into simple things like beads and, later, much more ambitiously, into glass vessels. To say that one of the earliest datable glass vessels (which is in the British Museum) is a small glass jug bearing a cartouche of Thotmes III (1501–1447 BC) gives just some idea of the great antiquity of glass.

Having progressed to the stage of making glass vessels, the ancient Egyptians produced some very beautiful work, quite elaborately decorated. They knew nothing of blowing glass and, instead, had to mould the molten glass round a solid core. The core was probably made of mud mixed with something like straw which had the effect of binding it. It was fixed to a metal rod and was fashioned into the required shape. Then it was coated with molten glass by means of trailing threads of glass round and round it until the core was entirely covered. To achieve the distinctive 'combed' decoration – wavy lines of different colours – threads of different coloured glass were wound round the core and while these were still in a viscous state a tool was pulled across them so that the pattern of wavy lines resulted (see plate 54). When the glass had cooled, the hard core was scraped out and the vessel was then detached from the rod and finished by having rough edges ground off. All this sounds very difficult and complicated, but in fact vessels can be made quite quickly by the core-winding process. The Corning Museum of Glass at Corning, New York, has a filmed demonstration of core-winding and it is surprising to see how comparatively simple it must have been for a skilled glass craftsman to produce a good quantity of work by these primitive methods.

Glass in ancient Egypt was a luxury material and as well as being used in the manufacture of vessels, it was also combined with gold and other precious metals in the making of jewellery.

Not only is the discovery of glassmaking itself unrecorded, but so also is another discovery of great importance: that of glass blowing. Skilled though the Egyptians were in their use of glass, they were limited in design and output by their ignorance of the fact that glass could be blown. The discovery of blowing is thought to have taken place in Syria where a thriving glass industry had become established. The date is unknown but it is believed that the process was in use during the first century BC.

With the discovery of blowing, the way was clear for glass manufacturing to develop. Of course this was bound to happen, but progress was not continuous and there was a long period when little was done.

Roman Glass

Glassmaking in the Roman Empire spread over a wide area and centres of production were set up in many towns. Roman glass is often coloured due to the amount of impurities in the ingredients. These produce glass which has amber, green or bluish tints and can give very attractive results. Much Roman glass has a beautiful iridescence; this is not due to some manufacturing process but is the result of the glass having been buried for centuries in damp conditions. Among many methods of decorating glass, the Romans excelled in

159

engraving, mostly using techniques derived from lapidary work. The best known example of this is the Portland Vase in the British Museum. This is made of deep blue glass 'cased' with white glass. The outer layer of white glass was cut away to form a design. In some places it was entirely removed, revealing the blue base; in others it was ground down until it was thin enough for a delicate blue shadow to show through. This method is known as cameo engraving.

Frankish Glass

In the barbarous and uncertain times which followed the fall of the Roman Empire, glassmaking in the west began a period of decline. This was only to be expected because it was very much a luxury industry and prospered only when conditions of daily life were orderly enough for people to want objects of beauty in their homes. Most glasses of the Frankish period, which followed the break-up of the Roman Empire, were beakers – which seems suitable for what appears to have been a rather swashbuckling age. By comparison with glass of the Roman period, these were heavy and not at all elegant, but there was a lot of inventive decoration. The glass was mainly mould blown and the decoration was often formed by trailing threads of glass over the basic shape to make patterns, or by applying blobs of glass called prunts.

Syrian Glass

While glassmaking was going through such a lean time in the west, Syrian glass continued to develop in the more settled conditions which existed eastwards at that time. Syrian glass is delicate and graceful, and it is often lavishly decorated. In later centuries this Syrian, or Islamic, glass became very ornate indeed. Typical examples of this work are enamelled and gilded beakers made during the thirteenth century and ornate mosque lamps made during the following century.

Venetian Glass

In the west, glassmaking eventually came into its own by way of Venice. If asked what they think of as the greatest name in glassmaking, most people will at once answer 'Venice'. They may not have even a rough idea of the place occupied by Venetian glass in the general development of glass, but the word 'Venice' immediately conjures up an idea of beauty and excellence. The general feeling is that if anything is described as being Venetian glass then what more could be desired?

The Venetian glass industry has ancient origins and as long ago as the eleventh century, glass was being made in Venice. Because of its geographical situation, Venice was an important centre of communication and trade. It was on the direct trade route to the east and to destinations as far afield as China. Commercially this was very important and it also meant that Venetian glassmakers could be in touch with fellow craftsmen in other important centres of glassmaking, such as Alexandria and Syria. It is also likely that craftsmen from other countries found their way to Venice, bringing with them their own styles of design and decoration. By the thirteenth century, Venice had become not only a city of culture but had also grown extremely prosperous, mainly as a result of supplying provisions and transport to the crusaders, who made their way to the east by passing through Venice. All these various geographical and economic factors helped to create favourable conditions for the expansion of a luxury industry like glassmaking.

By 1291 the craft had increased so much that the furnaces of the numerous glasshouses in the city had become a serious fire hazard and it was decided to move the entire industry to the island of Murano, where it has been ever since. The Venetians were fully aware of their supremacy in the manufacture of glass and took rather drastic steps to keep their craftsmen. To ensure that they did not migrate elsewhere and take their skills and trade secrets with them, an order was passed forbidding them to leave Venice on pain of death.

It was only natural, though, that glass as distinctive as that produced in Venice would be copied elsewhere by craftsmen who possessed sufficient skill. This was helped to some extent by the attitude of the people of Altare, near Genoa, where a parallel glassmaking industry was developing. Glassworkers from France had settled there as long ago as the ninth century and, by contrast with the Venetians, they travelled and spread a knowledge of their craft. As a result, there was a demand far and wide for Venetian glass, or for glass made in the Venetian style.

How can that style best be described for the benefit of those who have no possibility of seeing the real thing? If it had to be summed up in just one word, I think the word would have to be 'decorative'. The shapes of the great variety of vessels that were made ranged from simple and graceful to fanciful and ornate. However, even the simplest, without any applied ornamentation, could be described as decorative because of the beauty of their proportions and the delicacy of the glass itself. All kinds of vessels were made: bowls, flat dishes (tazza), goblets, jugs. Some were of extreme simplicity and were made of either colourless glass by itself, or colourless glass with an added decoration of coloured glass. Some had a great froth of coloured glass decoration. There was much gilding and enamelling and, by the middle of the sixteenth century, diamond point engraving too.

Apart from the very distinctive and elaborate decoration associated with Venetian glass – and in this connexion most people think of the goblets with great 'wings' of coloured glass – there were other developments taking place in Venice. One was the invention of 'cristallo'. Since the beginnings of glassmaking there had been a perpetual search for a clear metal resembling natural rock crystal as far as possible. The nearest approach so far was Venetian cristallo and it can probably be regarded as the first step towards the much later discovery of clear crystal. The same original ingredients for making glass were still used, but the Venetians realised that if manganese were added this acted as a decolourising agent. The resulting cristallo, as it was called, was rather greyish when thick but when it was thinly blown it became increasingly colourless. Perhaps this is one reason why so much Venetian glass is so thin.

The other characteristic development made by the Venetians was the production of decorated glass known as latticinio. Thin threads of opaque glass, either white or coloured, were incorporated in vessels made of clear glass. The vessel was blown and fashioned in such a way that the opaque threads spread out to form intricate and perfectly symmetrical patterns of spiralling or criss-crossing lines. Latticinio really is a marvel of the glassmaker's art.

In addition to the development of cristallo and the making of latticinio, the Venetians also became particularly known for reviving the art of making mosaic (or millefiori) glass, originally made by the Egyptians and Romans.

162

By the sixteenth century, Venetian glass was in great demand in foreign countries and when you think of the difficulty of transporting such delicate wares by the means then available, must surely have been one of the status symbols of the time. I always feel that these highly skilled glass workers must have derived great satisfaction from their craft, producing as they did such delicate and beautiful work. It almost seems as if they were enjoying to the full all that welter of applied decoration and asking themselves 'how much farther dare we go with this one – perhaps just another flourish'!

The Venetian glass industry was at its peak during the sixteenth and seventeenth centuries, but by the eighteenth century it was already in decline. Glass in the Venetian style (*façon de Venise*) was being made in many other places in Europe by then and Venice itself was no longer supreme.

German and Bohemian Glass

The description 'German glass' is usually applied to glass belonging to a rather wider area of northern Europe than present day Germany, since the style was also used in Bohemia.

While Venetian glassmaking was developing along lines which produced the characteristic delicacy already described, German glass was going in quite another direction. It was made more for everyday use, not for display, and the more solid designs were better suited to the less sophisticated society for which they were intended. German glassmaking survived the upheavals of the Dark Ages to some extent and glass continued to be made in numerous small glasshouses. These were hidden away in the forests where the essential wood for fuel was readily available. Glassmaking tended to run in families and each family tried to keep the secrets of its methods of work to itself.

For many centuries German glass had a colouring of various shades of brown, green or yellow. This was not intentional but was due to the impurities in the ingredients. It did not affect the designs of the glasses so there was no need to eliminate this attractive natural colouring.

As time passed, German glassware became less crude in shape, and by the fifteenth and sixteenth centuries it had a very recognisable style, reaching its peak in the seventeenth century. The main output was of drinking vessels of all kinds. These were thick and sturdy but the soft natural colours of the glass gave them great charm, and, as with many functional things, the shapes themselves were pleasing. The glasses were obviously designed for everyday use and appear in many paintings of the Dutch school portraying domestic life of the period. One distinctive style of decoration had developed: that of applying blobs of molten glass to the stem or bowl of the vessel to form patterns.

A famous design is a drinking glass known as a Roemer. This is a large glass which became very popular and was much used for Rhenish wine. It is usually thick and the sturdy appearance of the wide stem makes both glass and stem well suited to decoration with prunts. It was obviously designed for hard, daily use – a glass to be grasped rather than held delicately. The German Roemer is thought to be the forerunner of the rummer which became so popular in England in the nineteenth century.

German glassmakers also produced another well-known shape – the Humpen. This was tall, with straight sides. Humpen sometimes had lids and were often notable for their size, which could be huge. This made them particularly suitable for all kinds of decoration. Enamelling was frequently applied to Humpen and, apart from heraldry, many designs were lively scenes from everyday life. There was plenty of room on a Humpen! The Germans obviously liked decoration on their glass because later on much of it was engraved. This is dealt with in the chapter on the development of glass engraving.

In the seventeenth century there was considerable interest in coloured glass and a chemist, Johann Kunkel, developed a range of colours. His most famous invention, and the most sought after, was known as his ruby glass, which he obtained by using gold chloride.

In their search for ever more decoration, the German glassmakers also revived two Roman techniques. One was the method of sandwiching a layer of gold, which had been engraved through and back-painted, between two layers of clear glass. The other was the Roman method of glassmaking and engraving which had been used to make the Portland Vase. However, the German method was slightly different. After coating a vessel made of clear glass with an outer layer of coloured glass, they then cut right through the coloured outer layer with sloping cuts so that the clear glass was exposed along the lines of the cuts. This method of work involved using a technique associated with cut glass, whereas in the case of the Portland Vase the cutting (or engraving) was done with a wheel engraving technique which pared the outer casing down to various thicknesses as well as wholly removing it in some areas. The German method is known as flashed glass, and this is still very popular today on the Continent of Europe.

English Glass

The progress of English glassmaking remained rather obscure until early in the thirteenth century and before that it does not appear to have been very flourishing. This state of affairs was noted by the Venerable Bede who wrote that in the year AD 674 glassmakers had had to be summoned from Gaul in order to make glass for the windows of a church and monastery at Wearmouth.

However, things began to change from 1226 onwards because in that year a French glassmaker named Laurence (known as Laurence Vitrearius – the glassmaker) came to England and settled in the village of Dyers Cross near Chiddingfold in Surrey. This was an ideal situation for his work as it was on the edge of the Weald, in those days a great forest, and he thus had a good supply of wood for both fuel and potash. His enterprise obviously developed very successfully because by 1240 he was making windows for Westminster Abbey, then under construction. Laurence's son, and other glassworkers from France, also settled in the area which became a centre for glassmaking. The industry continued to develop and prosper for several hundred years, suffering only a temporary setback towards the end of the sixteenth century when many glasshouses were closed because they were using too much wood. The wood was needed for shipbuilding.

At about that time some immigrant glassmakers from Lorraine and Venice arrived. These were headed by Jean le Carré, who established a successful glasshouse in London, at Crutched Friars. When le Carré died in 1572 his glasshouse was taken over by a Venetian, Jacopo Verzelini, who had worked with him at Crutched Friars. However, two years later a mysterious fire totally destroyed the glasshouse. Far from being crushed by this, Verzelini started again and opened a new glasshouse. Within a few months, on 15 December 1575, he was granted a patent by Queen Elizabeth for twenty-one years, enabling him to make glass in the Venetian manner and to teach. By prohibiting imports of glass, the patent also gave him a monopoly. Only a few pieces of his glass now remain. These are all diamond point engraved and are thought to be the work of another Frenchman, Anthony de Lisle.

After the death of Verzelini in 1606, English glassmaking came under the control of a series of men who knew little or nothing of the techniques of glassmaking but were involved in the industry solely from a commercial standpoint. However, an important development was the growing use of coal instead of wood for heating the furnaces. In any case, the use of wood was forbidden from 1615 onwards so an alternative fuel was a necessity.

In the period dating from 1673 one of the really great discoveries in glassmaking took place. George Ravenscroft had been engaged by the Glass Sellers Company to work on research into making clear crystal. This had been the dream of glassmakers for so long and in spite of the development of cristallo by the Venetians the ideal glass had still not been achieved. At first, Ravenscroft was experimenting with ground, calcined English flints which he used as silica to replace imported pebbles from Venice. This gave rise to the description 'flint glass', although Ravenscroft soon went back to using sand. He also experimented with the addition of small quantities of lead in the form of lead oxide. However, he encountered one great problem with his early attempts to make clear crystal. This was known as 'crizzling' and was the breakdown of the glass into a maze of tiny cracks. Eventually, by using increased quantities of lead, the defect of crizzling was finally overcome and by 1676 the Glass Sellers Company was able to make a public announcement that its glass was now free from faults. So Ravenscroft had at last succeeded in making crystal, with a clarity and brightness never before achieved: lead crystal. This could be made in any thickness; the thickest crystal still retained its lustre and was as clear and colourless as the thinnest.

The beauty of the new material and the changing tastes of the age led, by the eighteenth century, to plainer designs of glass vessels. Applied exterior decoration by way of added glass was used less and less and finally vanished altogether. Emphasis moved to the shapes of the vessels themselves. Stems of wineglasses and goblets of all kinds became very varied; knops were used on them, airtwists were put inside, and some stems were faceted or had tears embedded in them. Variations were made to feet; sometimes they were domed, sometimes folded or conical. The shapes of bowls of wineglasses, too, varied greatly during the course of the century, and although the shapes themselves were without applied glass decoration, they were often engraved.

In the second half of the eighteenth century deeply coloured glasses became very popular and the famous Bristol blue dates from this period.

The early nineteenth century saw another typically English development in glass: this time by way of decoration, not of manufacture. This was cut glass which became, and has remained, very popular. The glass itself had to be rather thick and it was then given mitre cuts (grooves cut out in V-sections and intersecting at various angles). The cuts were used to form set patterns and the effect of the cutting on the clear crystal reflected light in a way that was not hitherto possible.

French Glass

Glassmaking in France did not become internationally important until the nineteenth century, although glass had been made there since Roman times. Early French glass, mainly drinking vessels, was made in the Seine-Rhine area. The designs were robust rather than graceful and the glass itself was not of very good quality. Ash from bracken was used in its manufacture and the glass was known, therefore, as *verre de fougère* (bracken glass). However, stained glass was also being made and was presumably well known because, as already mentioned, the Abbot of Wearmouth sent to France for glassmakers to glaze the windows of his church and monastery.

In later centuries, France became known for some technical developments in the making of glass. During the seventeenth century a new method of making sheet glass by casting was in use. In the same century, the manufacture of mirrors was, for a time, successfully carried on. This was largely because of the need for mirrors in the Palace of Versailles. In the eighteenth century, when coloured glass was so popular, the best known French manufactures were the paperweights made by the factories of Baccarat and Clichy.

One of the best known names in French glass is that of Emile Gallé.

He worked in the latter part of the nineteenth century and is known for his highly inventive use of decoration on glass.

Netherlandish Glass

Taking modern Holland and Belgium as one unit, as they once were, and thinking of them as the Netherlands, the glass produced by this area was much influenced by the Venetian style. In the middle of the sixteenth century a glasshouse producing Venetian-style glass was founded in Antwerp and its output became famous. In the seventeenth century, German influence was to the fore and led to the widespread production of Roemers in the German style. Later, glass in the English style was produced. The Netherlands were much influenced by other popular styles in the manufacture of glass but their major contribution to glass as a whole was by way of engraving. This is more fully dealt with in Chapter 1.

American Glass

In a small book published by the Corning Museum of Glass, Jane Shadel Spillman states that glassmaking was America's first industry. This new industry certainly had an uphill task in its early days. It suffered damaging restrictions imposed by English laws and several early attempts to establish glasshouses failed. However, in the first half of the eighteenth century an immigrant from Germany, Caspar Wistar, set up a glasshouse in New Jersey which did succeed. It is interesting to note that the glass produced was for windows and bottles – and hard to imagine two items more urgently needed in a new continent. Following upon the success of Wistar, another German immigrant, Henry Stiegel, established three other glasshouses. Shortly after the foundation of the Republic yet another German, John Frederick Amelung, started glassmaking at New Bremen in Maryland and produced some of the best glass that had been made in America.

After difficult beginnings, glassmaking in America did finally get going from 1790 onwards. The Republic was by then well founded and British restrictions on the manufacture of glass were lifted. It had always been hard to find sufficient trained immigrant glassblowers in America and, spurred on by this and also by the wish and need to speed up production, the process of pressing glass was developed. This was a major American contribution to the glass industry. For pressed glass a mould is used. The method differs from that used in mould-blown glass in that in press moulding a gather of glass is placed in a mould and a plunger is dropped down into the mould, pressing out the glass. The patterns on the mould imitated those used in cut glass, with delightful results. Until 1840 the designs were extremely intricate and covered almost the whole surface of the glass. In many cases they had the appearance of fine lace and were very delicate and attractive.

Towards the end of the century the greatest innovation in the design of glass was that introduced by Louis Comfort Tiffany. Tiffany had been trained as an artist but while travelling in Europe he had been much influenced by the art nouveau glasswork of Emile Gallé. He became particularly interested in design and founded a firm which produced coloured glass and other decorative items. He is known not only for his art nouveau designs, but also for his work in producing iridescent glass. He sought to recapture, by modern methods, the iridescence found in much Roman glass, Tiffany's new iridescent glass was known as Favrile glass. The shapes were graceful and simple, and today surviving examples are collectors' pieces.

The greatest name in contemporary American glass is undoubtedly that of Steuben. So firmly established in the public mind today, the company nevertheless has a rather chequered history. It is situated in south-western New York State in the town of Corning and was founded there in 1903 by an English glassmaker named Frederick Carder who had gone to Corning in order to design and make glass for T. G. Hawkes' Glass Company. Carder's aim was to produce art glass in different shapes and colours. During World War I, however, another company in Corning, the Corning Glass Works, needed extra furnaces to help in the production of technical glass which was in great demand at the time. To meet this situation the company bought the Steuben Glass Works and adapted the Steuben furnaces so that they could be used to manufacture technical glass needed for the war effort. When the war ended, the Corning Glass Works created the Steuben Division of Corning Glass Works, and the division reverted to the original Steuben Company's manufacture of art glass.

For several years Steuben produced a great variety of glass shapes, many of which were engraved. But although the glass was of a high quality, its style was not one which made it immediately recognisable as coming from any particular manufacturer. During the depression of the early thirties, things were not going altogether well for Steuben and there were some unsuccessful attempts at reorganisation. By 1933 Corning Glass Works was even considering closing its Steuben Division and ceasing to make art glass. Fortunately, at this point Arthur Amory Houghton Jr, a great-grandson of the founder of the Corning Glass Works and also one of its directors, assumed responsibility for the division and proposed new methods for running it. His suggestions were accepted by the other directors, a new company was formed and he became chief executive. This new venture has been described as 'a highly visionary approach to fine glassmaking', as anyone who has seen this splendid glass would agree.

Arthur Amory Houghton Jr decided to concentrate on two aspects of glassmaking: design and the quality of the material itself. To deal with the first, he brought into the company an architect, John Monteith Gates, and a sculptor, Sideny Waugh, and so began the Steuben tradition of using artist/designers to create works of art in glass. Throughout the years many internationally famous artists, both painters and sculptors, have been commissioned to create designs to be engraved by Steuben craftsmen. The quality of the glass was perfected by the parent company in 1932 and this, combined with the skill of the craftsmen themselves, provided the basis on which the new Steuben venture was built.

Today Steuben glass holds an unrivalled position. I always think of it as being mobile. To me, it conveys more than any other crystal the fact that glass has at some stage had a movement of its own – unlike potter's clay, for example, which is itself immobile until it is moulded into a shape, glass is a thickly flowing material. A piece of Steuben glass, if looked at fleetingly, gives the impression that it has only paused for a moment. If you don't look at it this very minute you might find that it has moved on!

The production of one of Steuben's major pieces of engraved glass can take a considerable time – perhaps even months – which is one reason why such works are either unique or made in very small quantities. They have great prestige and are given by successive presidents as official state gifts. In addition, they appear in museums and private collections all over the world.

Glass Manufacture Today

Even in this highly industrialised age an amazing amount of glass is still handmade – each piece being individually blown and fashioned by hand. At first sight, a modern glassworks presents a scene of seeming chaos and disorder. Groups of people are constantly moving about within limited areas; furnaces are glowing; hot glass is passed from one worker to another. But this is done rhythmically, without pause and always in the same direction. Every stage in the complicated production of a piece of glass is totally controlled and deftly done. It has to be because the glass from the molten mass in the pot is still at a temperature of 1100°C. So the chaos is highly organised.

Before the glass has reached the stage of being worked into shapes it is in the form of the same raw materials that have been used for thousands of years: sand, lime and soda – or, in the case of lead crystal, the addition of lead oxide. For the manufacture of much industrial glass, where colourless glass is not the aim, it does not matter if the sand contains impurities such as iron, but in the making of fine domestic glass or crystal the impurities must first be washed away. Each glasshouse has its own mix of raw materials.

Glass is still melted in clay pots. These are grouped round a central furnace and have walls about 8cm (3in) thick. They are not very large, often being about 80cm (2½ft) high and 115cm (3½ft) in diameter. The pots do not last long, an average time being three to eight weeks, and their replacement is a difficult operation. Before being used to fuse glass, a new pot is heated up slowly for a week to a temperature of 1100°C. The ingredients, after being weighed and carefully mixed, are known as a batch; the batch is then put into the pots. Any broken glass which has been removed from old pots, broken during manufacture or rejected as being imperfectly shaped, is added to the ingredients. These broken pieces are known as cullet. The batch and cullet can either be put into new pots or added to glass that is already molten in order to replenish the supply. In either case it takes ten hours to become molten when heated to a temperature of 1430°C.

Glassblowers work in teams, each team being grouped round a furnace; the exact composition of a team varies with individual glasshouses. Glassmakers' tools are varied: moulds made of graph-

171

ite, steel and wool, steel blowing pipes, shears and callipers, and wooden scoops and buckets.

Mr Jan Mollmark, managing director of Dartington Glass Ltd, has kindly provided the following description of the stages in making a wineglass, and also the methods used in making jugs, tankards and decanters. For a wineglass:

A gatherer takes the melted glass from a clay pot inside the furnace, knowing from experience how much glass to gather on the blowpipe end. Then it is marvered*on a smooth cast-iron plate and some air will now be blown into the pipe and a bubble will be formed. The pipe is now passed on to the next member of the team who will again gather more glass on to the bubble which has already been made. The new gather from the furnace will again be formed and blown into a mould which will shape the glass to the right shape. The mould is usually made from alder wood, cast-iron or graphite.

The blown glass is now passed on to the master blower who will shear on another molten piece of glass from another gatherer. This molten piece will be formed to a stem by the master blower. Again, the blown glass and the newly-formed stem is passed to the next member of the team – the footmaker – who will once more shear on another molten piece to the stem for the forming of the foot, which is done by the deputy master. At Dartington Glass a team which makes wineglasses contains seven or eight people with different skills.

The difference between making wineglasses and jugs, tankards and decanters, is as follows:

Wineglasses are blown with surplus glass between the rim and the blowpipe, and this surplus glass is ground off and finished in the finishing department (grinding room) when the glass has been cooled (annealed). Jugs, tankards and decanters are blown in a similar way to wineglasses, with a surplus amount of glass, but to remove the surplus glass in the case of these items you have to use the punting rod. When the items have been blown

---

* To 'marver' is to roll a blob of glass, attached to the blowing iron, up and down on a flat surface in order to get the required shape.

the punting rod is fastened to the bottom of the item and the blowing pipe can now be removed. The top ends of these jugs, tankards and decanters (in fact, the surplus glass) are then heated up in a small, very hot, moveable furnace known as a glory hole. The surplus glass is then sheared off by a specially made shear and the master blower forms the item to the right shape. If the item is a jug or tankard it is then passed on to the deputy master, who again shears on another molten piece of glass for the handle. All glass made in the blowing room is then passed through a special furnace, known as a lehr, which gradually takes down the temperature. This cooling process lasts anything from four to ten hours, depending upon the thickness of the glass. The cooling is known as annealing, and at the start of the process the temperature of the glass is 500°C. This is slowly reduced to room temperature. A slow cooling, or annealing, process is essential in order to avoid tension in the glass. If the cooling is done too quickly cracks could result. After annealing, the glass is finally finished in the finishing room. Decanters are individually fitted with stoppers, and open-mouthed pieces such as vases etc, are ground and polished by hand.

Stem-ware such as sherry glasses, wineglasses and goblets have the surplus glass removed in the finishing room. The surplus glass is cracked off from the rim after it has been marked with a diamond. The mark is heated up by a sharp flame whilst the glass rotates, and the force of the heat makes the glass crack where the diamond scratch mark is made.

During the next stage the glass is ground and finally top melted. Top melting is a process which melts the very edge of the glass and gives it a smooth finish. The glass is now ready for final inspection and packing.

Designs to Trace

The following designs, which have been produced by permission of Dover Publications Inc, New York, NY, USA, may be helpful to beginners as subjects which can be traced easily.

These could be used in conjunction with initials or monograms.

From *Handbook of Early Advertising Art* Dover Publications Inc.

Initials could be placed in this.

From *Japanese Design Motifs*, Dover Publications Inc.

From *Art Nouveau Designs in Color*, Dover Publications Inc.

From *Art Nouveau Designs in Color*, Dover Publications Inc.

177

From *Art Nouveau Designs in Color*, Dover Publications Inc.

Appendix

Some suppliers of tools and equipment

UK

Diamond and tungsten carbide hand tools
Lunzer Lancer: Mary Whitehead Ltd, Penfolds, Sandrock, Haslemere, Surrey GU27 2DN; Dubbeldee Diamond Co, 44–46 Halton House, 20 Holborn, London EC1N 2JD; Taranto Diamond Products Ltd, Unit B, Andrews Road, Mare Street, Hackney, London E8 4QN; van Moppes (Diamond Tools) Ltd, Winchester Road, Basingstoke, Hampshire RG22 4AJ. Shaw Abrasives (Diamond) Ltd, Waterloo Road, London NW2 7UN.

Unmounted tungsten carbide points and holders
Wimet Ltd, Torrington Avenue, PO Box 63, Coventry CV4 9AD.

Flexible drive drills and bench supports
John Quayle Dental Manufacturing Co Ltd, Deroter House, Dominion Way, Worthing, West Sussex BN14 8QN; Panadent Ltd, 15 Great Dover Street, London SE1 4YW.

Diamond and carborundum dental burrs and wheels, polishing wheels and tips
John Quayle Dental Manufacturing Co Ltd, Deroter House, Dominion Way, Worthing, West Sussex BN14 8QN; Panadent Ltd, 15 Great Dover Street, London SE1 4YW.

Sandblasting equipment
John Quayle Dental Manufacturing Co Ltd, Deroter House, Dominion Way, Worthing, West Sussex BN14 8QN.

Flock paper, cardboard presentation boxes, glass blanks, most tools
Wealden Glass Ltd, 27 Tarrant St, Arundel, West Sussex.

Etchall etching paste, abrasive powders, most tools
West Sussex Craft Supplies Ltd, Long Meadow, The Lane, Chichester
PO19 4PY.

Craft shops
Glass Etching Kit (Manufacturers: A. T. Lee & Co Ltd, 236a North End
Road, London W14)
Deka transparent glass paints
Protective masks (Manufacturers: Martindale Protection Ltd, Neasden
Lane, London NW10 1RN).

Toughening process for glass
If you fail to find a firm to undertake this, information may be obtained
from:
The Information Officer, Glass and Glazing Federation, 6 Mount Row,
London W1.

USA
Diamond and tungsten carbide hand tools
Lunzer Lancer: Lunzer Industrial Diamonds Inc, 48 West 48th Street, New
York, NY 10036.

Deka transparent glass paints
Distributors: Rupert, Gibbon & Spider, 470 Maylin Street, Pasadena, California 91105.

Etchall etching paste
Manufacturers: Etchall Inc, Columbia, Missouri 65201.

Australia
Diamond and tungsten carbide hand tools
Lunzer Lancer: Enquiries to: Lunzer Industrial Diamonds Inc, 48 West 48th
Street, New York, NY 10036, USA.

Deka transparent glass paints
Distributors: Search for Leisure Ltd, Gladesville 2111, NSW.

Where to see hand-engraved glass

The following list of museums can include only a few of those which have hand-engraved glass in their collections, although museums cannot always display everything in their possession.

UK
Aberdeen Art Gallery
Birmingham City Museum and Art Gallery
Royal Scottish Museum, Edinburgh
Glasgow Museum and Art Gallery
Laing Art Gallery, Newcastle
Plymouth City Museum and Art Gallery
Pilkington Glass Museum, St Helens
Cecil Higgins Art Gallery, Bedford
Ashmolean Museum, Oxford
Fitzwilliam Museum, Cambridge
Victoria and Albert Museum, London
British Museum, London.

USA
Wadsworth Atheneum, Hartford, Connecticut
Metropolitan Museum of Art, New York, NY
Art Institute of Chicago
Toledo Museum of Art
The Wine Museum of San Francisco
Museum of Fine Arts, Boston, Massachusetts
Chrysler Museum, Norfolk, Virginia
Philadelphia Museum of Art
Corning Museum of Glass, Corning, New York
Cleveland Museum of Art
Old Sturbridge Village, Sturbridge, Massachusetts
The Study Gallery, Douglas Hill, Maine.

Canada
Royal Ontario Museum (after 1982).

Australia
National Gallery of Victoria.

South Africa
South African Cultural History Museum, Cape Town.

Books for further reading

Brooks, John A., *Glass*. Hampton House Productions (1978)
Coppen-Gardner, Sylvia, *A Background for Glass Collectors*. Pelham (1975)
Crompton, Sidney, (ed), *English Glass*. Ward Lock (1967)
Heddle, G. M., *A Manual on Etching and Engraving Glass*. Alec Tiranti (1961)
Hughes, G. Bernard, *English Glass for the Collector*. Lutterworth Press (1967)
Lloyd, Ward, *Investing in Georgian Glass*. The Cresset Press (1969)
Mariacher, Giovanni, *Glass from Antiquity to the Renaissance*. Hamlyn (1971)
Savage, George, *Glass*. Weidenfeld & Nicholson (1965)
Weiss, Gustav, *The Book of Glass*. Barrie & Jenkins (1971)
Whistler, Laurence, *The Image on the Glass*. John Murray (1975)
Whistler, Laurence, *Pictures on Glass*. Cupid Press (Limited edition 1972)
Wills, Geoffrey, *Antique Glass for Pleasure and Investment*. Gifford (1971)
Wills, Geoffrey, *The Country Life Pocket Book of Glass*. Country Life (1966)

Information on the Guild of Glass Engravers can be obtained from:
The Secretary, Guild of Glass Engravers, c/o The Federation of British Craft Societies, 43, Earlham St, London WC2H 9LD.

Acknowledgements

To mention individuals and organisations in recognition of help they have so willingly given me could not possibly do justice to the kindness of so many people. Everyone, and every body, from whom I have asked information or guidance has responded with great generosity. However, among so many who have given help I should like to mention some in particular.

I should first of all like to thank David Peace for so kindly writing the foreword to this book and giving me valuable advice. I am very grateful to all those who have allowed me to write about them and their work in Chapter 6 and to those who have provided me with photographs of their engraving. Ian Gorf has been a great support in every aspect of the illustrations – not only photographing my own engravings but doing a considerable amount of other photographic work. Denis Bustard contributed a detailed account of his method of making presentation boxes for engraved glass. Jan Mollmark, Managing Director of Dartington Glass Ltd, supplied an account of the way glass is manufactured today, and Michael Farish, Information Officer of the Glass Manufacturers' Federation, and M. McCallum, Information Officer of the Glass and Glazing Federation, gave valuable technical information. Dwight Lanmon, Deputy Director, Collections, the Corning Museum of Glass, provided much valuable information about museum collections of glass in the USA. Dover Publications Inc, of New York allowed me to reproduce designs from some of their books and the Victoria & Albert Museum provided some illustrations of antique glass. As always, the staff of Bourne Hall Library, Ewell, were a great help, and innumerable friends supplied a great fund of information.

To all of them I should like to record my grateful thanks.

Index